ire
pretty fine (and
dandy) to me....
Mucho Amore!
Rodeo

To Rockstron,

How to be a Complete Dandy

also by Stephen Robins

The Importance of Being Idle
A LITTLE BOOK OF LAZY INSPIRATION

The Ruling Asses
A LITTLE BOOK OF POLITICAL STUPIDITY

How to be a Complete Dandy

a little guide for rakes, bucks, swells, cads
and wits

Stephen Robins

First published 2001 by
Prion Books Limited
Imperial Works, Perren Street,
London NW5 3ED
www.prionbooks.com

ISBN-1-85375-452-8

A catalogue record of this book can be obtained from the
British Library

Printed and bound in Great Britain by
Creative Print & Design, Wales

With great love and affection I dedicate this book to my grandmother Barbara for, inter alia, her exquisite propriety of dress.

CONTENTS

ACKNOWLEDGMENTS

The pictures on the following pages are reproduced courtesy of the Mary Evans Picture Library, London: 51, 67, 75, 81, 83, 96, 101, 107, 110, 119, 124, 126, 132, 139, 145, 148, 153, 159, 194.

Chapter 1
THE DANDY: A FORMAL INTRODUCTION

Dandyism is a complete theory of life ... It is a way of existing.

JULES BARBEY D'AUREVILLY

Dandyism may be taken as the art of selection, practised by a lover of the visible world.

DOUGLAS AINSLIE

Dandyism is almost as difficult a thing to describe as to define. Those who see things only from a narrow point of view have imagined it to be especially the art of dress, a bold and felicitous dictatorship in the matter of clothes and exterior elegance. That it most certainly is, but much more besides ... It is not a suit of clothes walking about by itself! On the contrary, it is a particular way of wearing these clothes that constitutes dandyism. One may be a dandy in creased clothes.

JULES BARBEY D'AUREVILLY

Dandyism is the last flicker of heroism in decadent ages.

CHARLES BAUDELAIRE

Precisely what is a dandy? Of course, we all know that a dandy is a clotheshorse, obsessed with the latest fashion – the cut of a coat or the length of a turn-up. But the dandy is not simply a walking mannequin or a narcissist besotted by his attire. Whilst clothes are important, it's not just about dressing up. If you have the attitude, you can be a dandy in rags.

From Beau Brummell to Andy Warhol, the dandy is someone who has turned himself and his life into a work of art. Rebellious style, cutting wit and debauched antics have always been the dandy's colourful calling cards. The great dandies of history gambled recklessly, drank to excess, lived beyond their means and chased young women relentlessly. From eccentric lords to street swells, from Regency bucks in their gambling clubs to decadent hedonists in their opium dens, the great dandies rank as some of the most enigmatic, most entertaining and most quotable personalities in history.

Every age has had its dandies, but the dandy as we know him was born in Regency England, the brainchild of a young man named Beau Brummell. In this era, the dandies strutted around the stage as the principal actors in the Theatre of Life. Throughout the nineteenth century, the part was rewritten time and time again as each successive generation created the dandy anew. The Bohemians, with their garish costumes, gave an exaggerated performance and turned life into the stuff of farce. They were followed by the fin-de-siècle Decadents who, revelling in depravity, saw life as a senseless tragedy. Their excesses turned it instead into black comedy. After the death of Queen Victoria, the Edwardian dandies hogged the limelight for a decade or two before the Bright Young Things sparkled on stage, with cocktails in their hands and clipped epigrams on the tips of their tongues, and life became an eccentric comedy once again.

The fact that the part has been rewritten countless times by numerous champions of dandyism ensures that the dandy is a multifaceted creature. If we look closely, however, and ignore the superficial differences, we can see a fixed and steady philosophy underneath. All dandies share the same outlook on life.

But what, I hear you ask, is dandyism?

Dandyism is an affected aesthetic philosophy of rebellion and leisure. Don't look so startled. It's really very easy to understand. Dandyism is affected in the sense of being unashamedly artificial and contrived. It is always a conscious pose. It is aesthetic, but the dandy smirks to himself as he transforms the aesthete's motto of 'art for art's sake' into his own motto of 'style for style's sake'. The dandy is an artist whose canvas is himself, the walking embodiment of the Wildean notion of the self as a work of art.

The dandy is rebellious in the sense of being nonconformist. He exhibits disdain for the fleeting ideas and transient tastes of his day. And because he needs something to react against, the dandy defines his era whilst defying it, personifying his times by subverting the prevailing expectations. The dandy is a rebel with no cause but himself.

Dandyism depends on leisure and the dandy must be a

committed idler, free from the humdrum entanglements of life that all too often interfere with style. The dandy does not work. He merely exists, ignoring morality, passion, ambition and the other mundane factors of human existence that usually stir a man to action. Instead he quietly cultivates an air of superiority and irresponsibility. He sneers as he sips his absinthe.

As an outward expression of inner beauty and innate superiority, dandyism is a means for a man upon whom the gods have bestowed exceptional qualities to prove his distinction from the common herd. Conceited? Of course, but arrogance is the dandy's birthright.

What, then, is the purpose of dandyism? Why does this outlook on life exist? Dandies are amusing and entertaining, and that's as good a justification for their existence as any other we may come up with, but there's more to it than that. The great dandies of history have all been outsiders. Be they cynical intellectuals, disenchanted artists or disaffected young men, they have all lacked a sense of integration. They have felt that mainstream society is unwilling to accept them. Some dandies have believed that the world has failed to appreciate their talents. Some have felt excluded on class grounds. Some have seen their religion or their sexuality as the cause of their exclusion. But whatever lies behind this sense of difference, dandyism has been the method used to gatecrash the visible world. Dandyism is both a pedestal on which to stand and a mask behind which to hide.

So the God of Dandyism demands that his followers

are more than animated tailors' dummies. Their clothes are simply the outward display of a complete attitude, symbolising control, independence, leisure, self-possession and free-thinking. Prepare to meet the followers, the philosophers and the high priests. Welcome to the Temple of Dandyism.

Chapter 2
THE RULES OF
DANDYISM

The following tenets, supported by inspiration and wit from its greatest practitioners, should be seen as the Little Red Book of Dandyism (although an other-worldly mauve would probably be more appropriate); the New Testament, the party manifesto, the ultimate commandments that any disciple of dandyism shall ignore at his peril. Read, commit to memory and put into practice with lashings of personal panache...

ARTIFICE

An alien abroad in the natural world, thou shalt worship at the altar of artificiality

The first duty in life is to be as artificial as possible. What the second duty is no one has as yet discovered.

OSCAR WILDE

To be smart is to be artificial. To be artificial is to be smart … To be artificial, and to be a little more improbable and impossible than one's neighbour, is to be a perfect success!

RONALD FIRBANK

Being natural is simply a pose, and the most irritating pose I know. To be natural is such a very difficult pose to keep up.

OSCAR WILDE

If you want a lesson in elaborate artificiality, just watch the studied unconcern of a Persian cat entering a crowded salon, and then go and practise it for a fort-night.

SAKI

LYING

Thou shalt tell falsehoods to create thine own truth

To tell you the truth, when I was at Oxford – I was bored. My impression of Oxford is that I sat in my rooms, bored, and that it ceaselessly rained. But now, warmed by their interest, I told them how I played soccer, rowed in the Eights, sat in the president's chair at the Union. Rank lies, of course. I cannot help it. I am like that – imaginative. I have a sensitive heart. I cannot get myself to disappoint expectations.

William Gerhardie, *The Polyglots*

There was once a woman who told the truth. Not all at once, of course, but the habit grew upon her gradually, like lichen on an apparently healthy tree … It began with little things, for no particular reason except that her life was a rather empty one, and it is so easy to slip into the habit of telling the truth in little matters. And then it became difficult to draw the line at more important things, until at last she took to telling the truth about her age … It may have been pleasing to the angels, but her elder sister was not gratified.

Saki, 'Reginald on Besetting Sins'

I was sitting in my drawing room drinking coffee and smoking yet another Turkish cigarette. The shutters were closed in defiance of the world outside, blocking out the strong summer sunlight that tortured my weary eyes. I was expecting an old friend, but I wasn't expecting him to be so jolly. Within seconds of walking through the door, he was insisting that the shutters be opened and the sunlight let in.

'Please,' I implored, 'have some consideration. I detest sunlight.'

'My dear fellow,' he drawled, 'it is truly delightful outside. Must you be so blind to the joys of nature?'

'Nature has no joys,' I replied with a scowl.

'How can you say such a thing?'

'The natural world is ugly. One only need glance at a landscape for its defects to become apparent. Nature is unpleasant. Rain, insects and mud are entirely without charm. Nature is vicious and nasty, with forests and jungles packed full of ill-tempered creatures indulging in all manner of unsavoury activities.'

'Like wolves?' my companion smirked.

'Well,' I mused, 'at least they realise what an awful world they inhabit and howl mournfully in self-pity.'

'But the Romantics delighted in nature.'

'Sentimental poppycock!' I proclaimed. 'Take any Romantic poet worth his salt, stick him in a pool of mud, shower him with a torrent of rain, fill his hair with spiders, and then ask him how much he cares for nature.'

'We may complain about the natural world,' my friend

said, 'but there's little we can do about it. We are part of it, after all, and it surrounds us.'

'We are not part of the natural world,' I insisted. 'We are part of an artificial world, a world of human creation.'

'What?'

'The artificial world,' I continued, 'is both the embodiment and the product of human civilisation. To be artificial is to be civilised. To be civilised is to be artificial. The totally artificial man is the zenith of human civilisation.'

'But the artificial,' my friend objected, 'is a tissue of lies.'

'Certainly,' I agreed, 'but what is wrong with artifice? Lying, my dear chap, is an art.'

'How can you say such a thing?'

'The liar, like the artist, aims to charm and to delight,' I said. 'He feels a responsibility to entertain his public. He brightens the dullest conversation. His listeners' needs are always at the forefront of his mind.'

'But what about the truth?' my companion complained.

'Just as the artificial is an improvement on nature,' I explained, 'fabrication is an improvement on lumpen reality. Lies are the new truth. Don't you find that it's hard to stick to mere facts when you have such wonderful powers of imagination at your disposal?'

'Certainly not.'

'I am surprised. I had always assumed that, were I to check, your stories would only rarely be corroborated by the truth. The idea that reports of your antics have a basis in reality alarms me considerably. Do you really stick to the truth?'

'Of course. I never lie. The very idea! What if I were to be found out? Just think of the social ramifications! The thought sends shivers down my spine.'

'Social ramifications indeed! Society is the biggest lie of all. It is entirely artificial. To be a success in society, you must become the most artificial of all social creatures – the dandy. You must create the fiction of yourself.'

'What do you mean?'

'You must be artificial, artificial to the core, artificial even when on your own. We dandies are all fictional. We are fabulous because we tell fables. We are perfect.'

'Well, we all feel better in the dark; now open the shutters.'

TASTE

Thou shalt trust wholly in thine own sensibilities

A dandy can never be a vulgar man.

CHARLES BAUDELAIRE

Good taste is better than bad taste, but bad taste is better than no taste.

ARNOLD BENNETT

Taste may be vulgar, but it must never be embarrassing. There is no need to embarrass anyone.

NOEL COWARD

Vulgarity is simply the conduct of other people.

OSCAR WILDE

What is exhilarating in bad taste is the aristocratic pleasure of giving offence.

CHARLES BAUDELAIRE

I was sitting in my drawing room, relaxing with a cup of Earl Grey after a particularly tiring visit to my tailor.

'Why on earth did you choose those trousers?' my companion asked, with a look of concern.

'Don't be rude,' I said.

'But they're pink!' he objected. 'I would like to see them cut to ribbons.'

'I don't care a jot for your opinion,' I said, raising my eyebrows. 'Taste is entirely subjective. It is its own explanation and its own justification.'

'What?'

'Good taste is an entirely subjective phenomenon,' I said. 'I define "good taste" as being everything that I like. Conversely, everything that you like is "bad taste" unless I agree with your preferences. Tell me, for example, why you are wearing velvet trousers.'

'Because I like them,' said my companion.

'They are the height of vulgarity.'

'Rot!' he exclaimed. 'My trousers are the very zenith of good taste.'

'Only from your point of view,' I said.

'So we may look disapprovingly at each others trousers, but we must hold our respective tongues?'

'Not at all. The subjectivity of taste shall not prevent me from denouncing your trousers.'

'In which case,' he said, 'I shall condemn yours in polemic verse.'

'And I shall write a rejoinder. A Petrarchan sonnet, I think, in praise of my *pantaloni*.'

'Tell me this first,' demanded my companion. 'If good taste and vulgarity can be the same thing subjectively, how are we to know, in the larger scheme of things, whether tastes are objectively good or bad?'

'Simple,' I said. 'Objective good taste is essentially a question of numbers. If a style is loved by many, we may presume that it is objectively vulgar. When a few influential members of society follow a certain style, we may presume that it is objectively good.'

'I can assure you that the vulgar masses will hate your new trousers. They may even riot in protest.'

'A riot! Splendid!' I exclaimed. 'Or a revolution, perhaps. That would be the perfect tribute to my good taste.'

'Your trousers and the masses would then be alike,' said my companion, archly. 'Revolting.'

ORIGINALITY

Thou shalt follow no path but thine own.

Dandyism is, above all the burning desire to create a personal form of originality, within the external limits of social conventions.

CHARLES BAUDELAIRE

A friend and I were dining in a splendid little restaurant in the heart of London. Neither of us had spoken for ten minutes, so intent were we on dissecting and consuming our chops.

'A penny for your thoughts,' I said suddenly. 'Better still,' I added, feeling gloriously extravagant, 'I'll make it a guinea.'

'What?' said my companion, looking somewhat startled. 'Sorry, old boy,' he added. 'I was thinking about something that you said the other day. You told me that vulgarity is essentially a question of numbers.'

'I'm glad you were listening to me,' I said. 'I never do.'

'You claimed that anything adored by the masses is objectively vulgar.'

'Yes,' I said. 'Anything that is "common" in the sense of being widespread is "common" in the sense of being vulgar.'

'But if a style is popular with the masses, one may consider it "normal". According to your principles, normality and vulgarity are one and the same.'

'True,' I said, taking a sip of my claret.

'In other words, in order to avoid being vulgar, one must always be original.'

'Yes. That makes perfect sense to me,' I said. 'What's your point?'

'If everyone were to be original, it would become "nomal" for a person's style to be unique. The quality of being unique would therefore become a vulgar quality.'

'Sophistry!' I asserted. 'How splendid!'

'What?'

'Your reasoning is fallacious. If a style is followed by one person alone, it cannot be deemed "normal". I maintain that the individual must create a personal form of originality in order to be truly stylish. One must always go against the grain.'

'But what would happen if other people aped this original style?'

'The style in question would become a fashion,' I replied.

'Presumably,' my friend said, 'that style would then be vulgar.'

'Why?'

'If it was "common" in the sense of being widespread,' my friend said, looking pleased with himself, 'it would be "common" in the sense of being vulgar.'

'If an original style is followed only by the Few,' I countered, 'it becomes an exclusive fashion and remains objectively good. If it is followed by the Many, on the other hand, it becomes objectively bad. That's why socialist principles can never be applied to fashion. One cannot redistribute "good taste"; it becomes "bad taste" in the process. One must always set fashions but never follow them.'

'I'm beginning to wish that I never listened to you,' my friend said. 'You're not making sense.'

'I do not claim to make sense,' I said. 'I claim only to be right.'

'I'm convinced that you're wrong. I refuse to believe that "good taste" can turn into "bad taste" in the way you describe. And originality is overrated. If I see a good idea, I copy it. Surely most people would be better copying good ideas instead of coming up with bad ideas of their own devising?'

'Better to have bad ideas than to have no ideas at all. Still, I'm glad that you have been using the old grey matter for once. I was beginning to think that your brain was under-used.'

'And I'm beginning to think that yours is over-valued,' declared my companion. 'Has anyone ever offered you a guinea for your thoughts? I thought not. I take it that you'll be paying for dinner tonight.'

We lapsed into silence for the second time that evening.

ORIENTALISM

Thou shalt covet the exotic, the outlandish and the forbidden; thy guiding light shalt be the East

The West has an absolute need to inject not only the colours of the East into its pallid spectrum of browns and greys and blacks but also its qualities of the bizarre and the alien.

Cecil Beaton

I confess that my Turkish prejudices are very much confirmed by my residence in Turkey. The life of these people greatly accords with my taste, which is naturally somewhat indolent and melancholy. And I do not think it would disgust you. To repose on voluptuous ottomans and smoke superb pipes, daily to indulge in the luxuries of a bath which requires half a dozen attendants for its perfection; … this is, I think a far more sensible life than all the bustle of clubs, all the boring of drawing rooms, and all the coarse vulgarity of our political controversies.

Benjamin Disraeli

The exotic, the outlandish and the alien tastes of the lands to the East are the perfect short-cut to originality – a short-cut known also as plagiarism, of course. But the dandy's love of all things Oriental is not merely stylistic. It is symbolic and philosophical. It represents a way of life rather than a way of accessorising. Elements of pure exotica represent the dandy's rejection of the norm. The Eastern outlook is incorporated into dandyism as a rebel philosophy with which to challenge the incumbent Western logic.

Dandies have often drawn on exotic influences, and the Near East has been as popular an inspiration as the Far East. Benjamin Disraeli enjoyed his visit to Turkey and loved to dress up in Turkish clothes, posing with an opium pipe in his hand. Byron asked his tailor to make him an elaborate Turkish costume with 'Full Trimmed Turban'. The dandy and aesthete Harold Acton went to China in 1932 with the aim of becoming an ambassador of hedonistic wisdom between East and West. There he cultivated for himself a Confucian serenity. The dandy photographer Cecil Beaton was also rather keen on the styles of the East, and the dandy novelist Ronald Firbank was utterly enchanted by foreign tastes and accents. A number of the fin-de-siècle dandies adopted the fez as a symbol of imported style.

STYLE

Thou shalt cultivate style as thine own substance

Style is knowing who you are, what you want to say, and not giving a damn.

Gore Vidal

In all unimportant matters, style, not sincerity, is the essential. In matters of grave importance, style, not sincerity, is the vital thing.

Oscar Wilde

Properly understood style is not a seductive decoration added to a functional structure; it is of the essence of a work of art.

Evelyn Waugh

The summer's afternoon in question held out no immediate prospect of pleasure or intrigue, so a friend and I decided to sit in the shade of a tree somewhere and polish off a few bottles of champagne. Our primary task was the acquisition of sufficient champagne. Fortuitously, my friend's uncle had a cellar full of the stuff. We opened a bottle and began to discuss our second concern: the location of the tree under which we would sit. After an hour's debate we settled on Hyde Park.

'The most stylish trees in London,' said my companion, 'are to be found in Hyde Park.'

'A tree,' I said, somewhat pedantically, 'can never be stylish. It can only be tasteful.'

'What are you complaining about?' he asked.

'People can be stylish,' I explained, 'but objects can only ever be tasteful.'

'Prithee, sir, continue.'

'Taste relates to one's choice of physical objects. Style relates to the way in which one uses those physical objects. To be stylish, one must express a quiet confidence in one's tastes.'

'What do you mean?' my companion asked.

'Let us use wine as an example,' I said.

'Talking of which,' he said, refilling our glasses, 'let's have a drop more champagne.'

'When we speak of wine,' I said, didactically, 'my taste relates to the variety of wine that I choose to drink. My style, on the other hand, relates to the way in which I drink it. It is not at all stylish, for instance, to drink one's wine in a boisterous manner at a vicar's luncheon.'

'You promised to stop ragging me about last Tuesday's little fiasco,' said my companion.

'Little fiasco?' I scoffed. 'It was more of a brawl.'

'The clergy should be more circumspect than to go around insulting people,' he said. 'It really wasn't the vicar's place to comment on my behaviour.'

'It wasn't your place to slap the vicar.'

'But I slapped him with style.'

'Which is more than can be said for the way in which you had been conducting yourself after lunch. But let us stop quarrelling. We must go to Hyde Park while the sun is shining. We shall snooze under a tree, drink champagne, and enjoy the admiration of passing girls. In their eyes, no doubt, we will appear to possess both perfect taste and perfect style. Terribly sophisticated, I'm sure. As long as you don't slap anyone, that is.'

SELF-LOVE

Thou shalt be the centre of thine own universe

I'm an enormously talented man, and there's no use pretending that I'm not.

NOEL COWARD

If egotism means a terrific interest in one's self, egotism is absolutely essential to efficient living.

ARNOLD BENNETT

There is only one thing in the world worse than being talked about, and that is not being talked about.

OSCAR WILDE

Eugene's a pedant in his dress,
In fact a thorough fop, no less.
Three whole hours, at the least accounting,
He'll spend before the looking-glass.

PUSHKIN, *Eugene Onegin*

I can take any amount of criticism, so long as it is unqualified praise.

NOEL COWARD

Egoist, n. a person more interested in himself than in me.

AMBROSE BIERCE

To love oneself is the beginning of a life-long romance.

Oscar Wilde

Few remember that the dandy's vanity is far different from the crude conceit of the merely handsome man. Dandyism is, after all, one of the decorative arts. A fine ground to work upon is its first postulate. And the dandy cares for his physical endowments only in so far as they are susceptible of fine results.

Max Beerbohm

He fell in love with himself at first sight and it is a passion to which he has always remained faithful. Self-love seems so often unrequited.

Anthony Powell

A narcissist is someone better looking than you are.

Gore Vidal

It is only the shallow people who do not judge by appearances.

Oscar Wilde

I was supping with a friend last autumn, talking about Roman architecture, when I made a remark of dubious veracity. My companion looked quizzical and challenged my learning.

'Are you sure?' he asked.

'I'm never sure about anything,' I replied, attempting to appear blasé. 'It's just pure chance that I'm always correct.'

'Egotism,' he winced, 'does not become the gentleman.'

'Fiddlesticks!' I exclaimed. 'Egotism is terribly important. There can be no happiness in this life without it.'

'Pride,' he warned, 'is one of the Seven Deadly Sins.'

'Deadly?' I queried. 'More people are killed by their virtues than by their vices. I am absolutely certain that no one has ever died of pride.'

'Deadly,' my friend repeated, 'and sinful.'

'If God disapproves of my high self-opinion,' I said, 'I shall be forced to plead justification.'

'Then the defence shall be more offensive than the crime.'

'In which case,' I said, 'I shall plead necessity. The artist cannot ignore his canvas. It is the focal point of his artistic endeavour. When the self becomes a work of art, egotism is an unavoidable by-product. The dandy's egotism is the artist's egotism.'

'It's no good appealing to aesthetics,' my friend commented. 'The artist's conceit is the world's least exciting form of arrogance.'

'The dandy's egotism,' I corrected, 'is not to be confused with primitive arrogance.'

'What's the difference?'

'Belief in one's self as a work of art,' I argued, 'is not the same thing as self-belief.'

'How delightful!' my friend laughed. 'Pride is to be excused on the grounds of vanity!'

'Not in the slightest,' I said. 'You miss my point. Narcissus fell in love with his own reflection, but the dandy falls in love with his own creation.'

'A superficial difference, I think.'

'No, my dear chap. Love of one's artificial self is entirely different from love of one's natural self.'

'Do be quiet, or I shall begin to hate your natural self and your artificial self.'

'My dear fellow, you mustn't be so petulant. Envy is a sin too, you know.'

IDLING

Thou shalt spend thy days in idleness

The Hero of elegant idleness – the Hero Dandy.

JULES BARBEY D'AUREVILLY

A dandy does not do anything.

CHARLES BAUDELAIRE

I was a luxurious personage in those days. I had a bath made from my own design; across it were constructed two small frames – one for the journal of the day, and another to hold my breakfast apparatus; in this manner I was accustomed to lie for about an hour, engaging the triple happiness of reading, feeding and bathing.

EDWARD BULWER LYTTON, *Pelham*

In order to be fashionable, one must enjoy rest without having experienced work ... Like steam engines, men regimented by work all look alike and have nothing individual about them. The man-instrument is a social zero.

HONORÉ DE BALZAC

To be a useful man has always seemed to me to be something quite hideous.

CHARLES BAUDELAIRE

Idleness is a glorious and noble way to spend one's days. Some unkind souls dismiss laziness as a waste of time, but they are much mistaken. The idler uses his time wisely and chooses not to fritter it away by wasting his hours in toil. Idleness leads to contemplation, creativity and inventiveness, which, in turn, resolve themselves in literature, philosophy, poetry, and every other component of 'civilisation' as we know it. The mind roaming free in idleness is a creative and unstoppable force. The dandy, sipping his absinthe in a café all afternoon, is likely to achieve more in the way of thought than the paid servant of toil, whose mind is shackled and distracted by anxiety.

One afternoon last summer, I was snoozing on the terrace in a leather armchair. I had persuaded a porter to move it outside, and I had been feeling rather pleased with my little triumph. The light summer breeze ruffled my hair and I was dreaming of caviar. Suddenly, I was rudely awakened by a friend. He suggested, in tones of utmost urgency, that we purchase some hammocks forthwith.

'What?' I said, still bewildered by sleep.

'Let's buy some hammocks,' he said again. 'We can string them up here, between these columns. We'll laze in our respective hammocks, smoke pipes, and look altogether dashing.'

'The hammock,' I said, regaining my composure, 'is an over-sentimentalised contraption. One must not romanticise the hammock. Lolling in a hammock is a most uncomfortable way of going about one's relaxation.'

'Really?'

'Last summer, I fell out of a hammock. The summer before, I got inexplicably tied up in one. And deckchairs can be pretty dangerous too. I knew a curate from Berkshire who was eaten alive by a deckchair. No, my dear fellow, you must choose an armchair if you want to unwind in safety.'

'Don't be a rotter,' he said. 'Let's buy hammocks! It'll be terribly good fun.'

'If you want to risk your neck in the pursuit of fun,' I said, 'you must go elsewhere. I am content to sleep here, in my armchair, in the sun.'

'Dash it all!' he muttered as he walked away. Soon I was asleep again, dreaming of champagne and roulette. I was rudely awakened by one of those sporty types. I had seen him around before, and I didn't much like the look of him.

'Hullo!' he grinned, holding out a hand in the hope that I would shake it. 'I'm Rufus.'

'Pleased to meet you, Rufus,' I said. After exchanging pleasantries, I closed my eyes again, hoping that he would go away. He didn't.

'We need someone else to play tennis,' he said. 'We were keen on playing doubles. Fancy a game?'

'My dear Rufus,' I said, opening my eyes, 'I hope that you won't be unduly disappointed by my refusal. I am keen on preserving my reputation as a dandy.'

'I'm sure that dandies play tennis sometimes.'

'Dandies,' I said, 'don't do anything at all. We simply exist. We have no duties, no cares and no ambitions. Why should I play tennis when I can choose not to?'

'Why do anything when you can choose not to?' he said, hoping that a rhetorical question would be answer enough.

'And I choose to do nothing,' I said with a weary look. 'Enjoy your game.'

I dozed until teatime.

HEDONISM

Thou shalt revel in the pleasures of excess

I believe wholeheartedly in pleasure.

NOEL COWARD

I have not been afraid of excess: excess on occasion is exhilarating. It prevents moderation from acquiring the deadening effect of habit.

W. SOMERSET MAUGHAM

Moderation is a fatal thing. Nothing succeeds like excess.

OSCAR WILDE

ENNUI

Thy decadent soul shalt be bored by simple pleasures

Dandyism is the product of a bored society.

JULES BARBEY D'AUREVILLY

The Tired Hedonists ... it is a club to which I belong.
We are supposed to wear faded roses in our buttonholes when we meet, and to have a sort of cult for
Domitian. I am afraid you are not eligible. You are too
fond of simple pleasures.

OSCAR WILDE

The dandy, as Baudelaire was well aware, was a kind of
worldly ascetic whose motto was *nihil admirari*, which,
properly understood, means 'never find anything interesting.'

ERIC GANS

I rather like bad wine. One gets so bored of good
wine.

BENJAMIN DISRAELI

Oscar Wilde's idea of a club for Tired Hedonists is one of the most dandified notions he ever came up with. The dandy is always a tired hedonist. He has over-indulged on simple pleasures and is consequently bored by them. Empathy is not one of my specialities, but here I empathise. Last week, in that desolate period between tea and dinner, I empathised very strongly indeed.

'I'm bored,' I announced.

'I'm tired of hearing you say that,' my companion said.

'You're bored by the fact that I'm bored? Cripes! It sounds contagious.'

'Then we must find a cure.'

'Why bother?' I said with affected despondency.

'We must find a cure before the entire population of London is infected by your *ennui*. We don't want to have an epidemic on our hands.'

'My dear fellow,' I said, 'I hope you're speaking in jest. You know that there is no cure for my boredom. It is one of the facts of life. I must suffer in silence.'

'If there is no cure,' said my friend, 'we must, at the very least, find enough palliatives to last until dinnertime.'

'Life's pleasures have no charm left,' I said. 'I've tried everything, and I've become bored by it.'

'Have you tried opium?' he asked.

'No, of course not!' I said. 'I'm a decent, law-abiding sort of chap.'

'Really? What a waste of potential!'

'Decent,' I reiterated, 'and law-abiding. You mustn't tell anyone, of course. It would ruin my reputation if people found out. The path to immortality is paved with immorality.'

'If boredom is your disease,' my friend pondered, 'perhaps the condition is its own cure.'

'What do you mean?' I asked.

'If boredom is the only thing that you find interesting,' he said, 'it could be made to eradicate itself.'

'I don't understand,' I said. 'What are you talking about?'

'Don't you see? You must become a scholar of *ennui*. Chronicle it through the ages. Examine it in literature. Become fascinated by boredom. No longer will it be a state of existence. Instead it will be a subject of inquiry.'

'A splendid idea!' I said. 'I shall go to the library immediately and read something boring. That'll do me the world of good.'

LUXURY

Thou shalt pursue a life of extravagance

The only thing that can console one for being poor is extravagance. The only thing that can console one for being rich is economy.

OSCAR WILDE

I am determined to travel through life first class.

NOEL COWARD

We cannot afford to do without luxuries.

OSCAR WILDE

Give us the luxuries of life, and we will dispense with its necessities.

J. L. MOTLEY

Let us all be happy, and live within our means, even if we have to borrow the money to do it with.

ARTEMUS WARD

All decent people live beyond their incomes nowadays, and those who aren't respectable live beyond other people's. A few gifted individuals manage to do both.

SAKI

The dandy must be extravagant. For him, luxuries are the new necessities. His tastes, being the most refined, will always be the most expensive. He is devoted to luxury. It is his god, and he worships this deity with the strictness and exactitude of a monk. But where the monk's life is austere, the dandy's is extravagant. Committed to enjoying the luxuries of life, he will do anything to obtain them – even if it means going without the necessities. The dandy would rather have caviar than bread. He would rather have a silk handkerchief than an overcoat. Being extravagant, of course, he will usually borrow enough money to ensure that he can afford both.

INTELLECT

Thou shalt use thy intellect as a toy not a tool, and thou shalt be cynical at all times

The only way to atone for being occasionally a little overdressed is by being always absolutely over-educated.

Oscar Wilde

If you take up an attitude – not an offensive attitude – of calm, conscious superiority and aloofness – security in your superior attainments and knowledge, you will get an enormous reputation as an intellectual.

Brian Howard

To be clever in the afternoon argues that one is dining nowhere in the evening.

Saki

A little sincerity is a dangerous thing, and a great deal of it is absolutely fatal.

Oscar Wilde

Cynicism is intellectual dandyism.

George Meredith

The dandy is always likely to be a cynic, castigating the world without advising it how to improve itself, for cynicism is the quickest and surest route to gaining a reputation as a man of intellect. Of course, the dandy is never a genuine intellectual. He will never slave away on intellectual or academic pursuits. He will never pore over books at his desk for hours on end. The dandy realises that the intellect is a thing of play, not a tool of work. The intellect works best when he is idle, so the dandy does not 'study'. Instead, he simply contemplates. Contemplation requires no effort beyond the ordinary and unavoidable working of the brain. Showy in everything, the dandy's learning is all superficial, and he is content to use more words than he needs to say more than he knows. Why bother developing a depth of knowledge when one can exhibit such impressive shallows?

WIT

Thou shalt cultivate a perfection in wit to match thy dress

Every sentence is an epigram, and every epigram slaughters a reputation or an idea.

ARTHUR SYMONS ON J. K. HUYSMANS

If a person isn't generally considered beautiful, they can still be a success if they have a few jokes in their pockets. And a lot of pockets.

ANDY WARHOL

'I expect you don't know me with my moustache,' said the newcomer; 'I've only grown it in the last two months.'
'On the contrary,' said Clovis, 'the moustache is the only thing about you that seemed familiar to me. I felt certain that I had met it somewhere before.'

SAKI, The Talking-Out of Tarrington

Epigrams are like buses: you don't see one for ages and then three arrive at once. Wit is more like trains: it tends to arrive late, if at all. The French have a phrase, *esprit de l'escalier*, to describe this phenomenon. It translates literally as 'the wit of the staircase' – all those amusing things that you did not say at the party which now pop into your head, as if from nowhere, as you descend the staircase on your way out. Perhaps we should follow Oscar Wilde's example and think of amusing things to say before we arrive.

There is, of course, nothing wrong with such artificiality so long as one appears to be entirely unaffected. You should always appear to be a natural wit. If you sit at home chewing epigrams, they should burst forth later as if spontaneous. If you cannot help but appear contrived, avoid quips altogether and follow Beau Brummell's example – be impertinent instead.

SNOBBERY

Thou shalt practise snobbery and look down on all others

Other people are quite dreadful. The only possible society is oneself.

Oscar Wilde

I am becoming almighty sick of the Welfare State; sick of general 'commonness', sick of ugly voices, sick of bad manners and teenagers and debased values.

Noel Coward

The dandy has often been accused of being a snob. And rightly so. Snobbery is, after all, the desire to remain distinct from the mass of ordinary mortals. This is traditionally thought of as the prerogative of the upper-classes, but it can work in reverse. After W. H. Auden's return from Berlin in 1928, Auden and his cronies deliberately 'proletarianised' themselves and shunned all things aristocratic. Auden took to wearing a flat cap, dropped his 'aitches', and ate peas with a knife. His friend Christopher Isherwood drank strong black tea by the gallon and ate mountains of chocolate with the aim of ruining his perfect teeth. Stephen Spender allowed himself to be cheated by unemployed workers, and Gabriel Carritt changed his name to Bill.

I can say, in all sincerity, that I am all in favour of whippets and pints of bitter. Last summer, however, a friend accused me of ridiculing the proletariat.

'I'm sure I would never be so snobbish,' I said. 'And besides, I would never stoop so low as to talk about the vulgar herd.'

'Snobbish? You? Never!' said my friend with a giggle.

'Snobbishness is not becoming,' I said. 'Only the *nouveau riche* are snobbish.'

'Well, you're entirely *nouveau* and not at all *riche*,' my friend announced.

'Pot? Kettle? Black? You're the most impecunious *parvenu* I've ever met.'

'Let's not argue,' my friend announced. 'We must count our blessings. At least we're not snobbish. And at least we're not common.'

UPWARD-MOBILITY

Thou shalt create thine own aristocracy of style

Dandyism flourishes especially in periods of transition, when democracy is not yet all-powerful and the aristocracy is just beginning to totter and fall. Amidst the turmoil of these times, a small group of men who are socially, politically and financially ill at ease – but all of them rich in determination – will conceive the idea of founding a new sort of aristocracy, stronger than the old for it shall be based on the most precious, the most indestructible factors, on the divine gifts that neither work nor money can give.

CHARLES BAUDELAIRE

For all their snobbishness, dandies are often society's newcomers. Like Beau Brummell, they may be extraordinary men of ordinary backgrounds. Like Noel Coward, they may often try to hide their bourgeois backgrounds behind upper-crust accents. Essentially, however, dandyism embodies a sense of superiority. Its social ideal is an aristocracy of taste and style. Dandyism's model of social superiority is based on the rule of the fashionable elite.

As Baudelaire first realised, dandyism is at once a reaction against traditional aristocracy and a development of it. His observation that it flourishes in periods of social transition may be too general to be universally accurate, but the notion does carry some force. When the old aristocracy of inherited wealth and title is unsettled, dandies spring up as pretenders to the throne. Literally, the word 'aristocracy' means 'rule by the best'. Dandies want to see rule by the best dressed.

This notion of superiority ensures that, in their own scheme of things, dandies always come out on top. They are superior to the vulgar masses whence they themselves sprang. They are superior to the vulgar nobility. Despite its apparent snobbery, dandyism rides roughshod over the normal class system. To be a dandy is to have class without belonging to one.

REBELLION

Thou shalt be a rebel with no cause but thyself; and perpetual rebellion shalt be thy lifeblood

Rebellion is part and parcel of dandyism: one of its objectives is outward appearance.

Albert Camus

All dandies share the same characteristic of opposition and revolt; all are representatives of what is best in human pride, of that need, which is too rare in the modern generation, to combat and destroy triviality. That is the source, in your dandy, of that haughty, patrician attitude, aggressive even in its coldness.

Charles Baudelaire

Albert Camus in *L'Homme Révolté* (translated as *The Rebel*) saw dandyism as the destructive, nihilist side of the Romantic revolt. As such, the dandy is a rebellious man. Camus argued that the dandy always creates his own unity by aesthetic means, and that this aesthetic is one of singularity and of negation. 'The dandy,' said Camus, 'is always in opposition. He can only exist by defiance.'

Until modern times, Camus claimed, man derived his coherence from God. As soon as man stopped defining himself in relation to his Creator, he could only be sure of his existence by finding it in the expression of others' faces. The dandy, therefore, derives his coherence from the public. Other people are his mirror. When the dandy is alone and without a mirror, he cannot be sure of his existence. 'For the dandy,' says Camus, 'to be alone is not to exist.' Human capacity for attention is limited, however, and it must be ceaselessly stimulated, so the dandy is always compelled to astonish.

The dandy, thought Camus, sets himself up in opposition to God. 'Dandyism,' he claimed, 'is always dandyism in relation to God. The individual, in so far as he is created, can oppose himself only to the Creator.' In short, dandyism inaugurates 'an aesthetic of solitary creators, who are obstinate rivals of a God they condemn.'

So perhaps the first dandy was in fact the devil, the original rebel cast from heaven to wander leisurely throughout the earth, banished for the sin of vanity after showing off about his dandified goatee one time too often. Maybe, on the other hand, the first dandy was Adam, a rebel cast from the Garden of Eden for the sartorial crime of clothing his nakedness with a rather natty and fetching fig leaf.

DRESS

Thou shalt look upon thyself as a work of art

One should either be a work of art, or wear a work of art.

OSCAR WILDE

Any man may be in good spirits and good temper when he's well dressed.

CHARLES DICKENS

The greatest of all science – the science of dress.

EDWARD BULWER LYTTON

Not until nudity be popular will the art of costume be really acknowledged. Nor even then will it be approved.

MAX BEERBOHM

A dandy is a clothes-wearing man, a man whose trade, office, and existence consists in the wearing of clothes. Every faculty of his soul, spirit, purse, and person is heroically consecrated to this one object, the wearing of clothes wisely and well.

THOMAS CARLYLE

Without black velvet breeches, what is man?

JAMES BRAMSTON

To clothe the body that its fineness be revealed and its meanness veiled has been the aesthetic aim of all costume, but before our time the mean had never been struck. The ancient Romans went too far. Muffled in the ponderous folds of a toga, Adonis might pass for Punchinello, Punchinello for Adonis. The ancient Britons, on the other hand, did not go far enough. And so it had been in all ages down to that bright morning when Mr. Brummell, at his mirror, conceived the notion of trousers and simple coats. Clad according to his convention, the limbs of the weakling escape contempt, the athlete is unobtrusive, and all is well.

MAX BEERBOHM

With an evening coat and a white tie, anybody, even a stockbroker, can gain a reputation for being civilised.

OSCAR WILDE

There is one other reason for dressing well, namely that dogs respect it, and will not attack you in good clothes.

RALPH WALDO EMERSON

FASHION

Thou shalt set fashions but never follow them

Fashion is what one wears oneself. What is unfashion-able is what other people wear.

OSCAR WILDE

One could perhaps divide the hierarchy of fashion into three ranks: those who play fashion's game and are the sheep; those who play the game and are the leaders; and, lastly, the real shepherds, who, though they avoid or eschew active participation, cannot help being fash-ionable because of the authority with which they express their tastes.

CECIL BEATON

In one way Dandyism is the least selfish of all the arts. Musicians are seen and, except for a price, not heard. Only for a price may you read what poets have written. But the dandy presents himself to the nation whenever he sallies from his front door. Princes and peasants alike may gaze upon his masterpieces. Now, any art which is pursued directly under the eye of the public is always far more amenable to fashion than is an art with which the public is but vicariously concerned.

MAX BEERBOHM

The dandy sees clothes as his primary means of imprinting himself on the memories of others. He loves to startle. He dresses to impress. But those others will follow where he leads. As mentioned elsewhere, the dandy sets fashions but never follows them. When the top hat first appeared in 1797, for example, several women fainted, dogs howled, children screamed and a young man's arm was broken in the stampede. The wearer was charged with inciting a riot. Eighteen years later, General Picton wore one at the Battle of Waterloo. By this time, of course, no dandy would be seen dead in one.

MONEY

Thou shalt always live beyond thy means

I'm living so far beyond my income that we may almost be said to be living apart.

SAKI

I don't want money. It is only people who pay their bills who want that, and I never pay mine.

OSCAR WILDE

They say that one always pays for the excesses of one's youth; mercifully that isn't true about one's clothes.

SAKI

Living in the lap of luxury isn't bad, except you never know when luxury is going to stand up.

ORSON WELLES

The dandy has a rather ambivalent attitude towards money. He loves to spend money, but he hates to earn it. He will resort to any scheme to drum up funds. To be a dandy, you must learn how to obtain money without working for it. Take Felix Krull, the protagonist of *Bekenntnisse des Hochstaplers Felix Krull* by Thomas Mann, for example. Felix is the son of a Rhenish manufacturer of sparkling wine of exceptionally poor quality. A young and good-looking lad, he creates for himself a personality to charm and deceive the wealthy elite, and to allow him to pursue a successful career in high society.

Felix finds an unusual means of evading service in the German army and heads for Paris. A 'misplaced' jewel case in French customs gives him a good beginning. With his ill-gotten gains, he buys new clothes and he becomes a dandy. He acquires 'a pair of handsome button shoes … three or four collars, a tie, a silk shirt, a soft hat … an umbrella that fitted inside the shaft of a cane … deer skin-gloves and a lizard-skin wallet … and an attractive suit of light, warm grey wool.' His charming appearance attracts the attentions of the literary wife of a rich manufacturer of lavatory fittings, and they have a brief but passionate affair.

Felix meets the Marquis de Venosta, a young aristocrat in love with a singer named Zaza. Venosta is in a spot of bother. His father disapproves of this affair and has arranged to send Venosta on a long excursion around the globe in order to allow him to forget his paramour. Felix persuades Venosta to swap roles with him. It seems like a good deal to both parties. The Marquis gets to continue his affair in Paris, and Felix gets to swan around the world posing as an aristocrat, supported by the ample funds of Venosta's father.

SPORT

Thou shalt not play sport

I'm afraid I play no outdoor games at all. Except dominoes. I have sometimes played dominoes outside
French cafés.

OSCAR WILDE

The dandy is proud of his impeccable appearance. Sport
can so easily undo all his good work. Most sporting activities have the annoying effect of making one break into a
sweat. One's immaculate hair is messed up. One's clothes
get dirty and crumpled. And besides, short trousers are terribly unflattering. As an idler by nature, the dandy would
rather stroll around town all day in a mood of tranquil
contemplation than sweat away on the tennis court or get
so very muddy on the rugger field.

The dandy might watch sport occasionally, particularly
if a wager is being placed on it, but when it comes to taking part he has neither the inclination nor the knowhow.
Give him a tennis racket, for example, and he stands there
looking bewildered and slightly upset. The young Disraeli,
famous as a dandy long before he became Prime Minister,
wrote about tennis is a letter to his friend Bulwer Lytton in
1830:

Yesterday, at the racket court, sitting in the gallery

among strangers, the ball entered, and lightly struck me and fell at my feet. I picked it up, and observing a young rifleman excessively stiff, I humbly requested him to forward its passage into the court, as I really had never thrown a ball in my life.

The dandy detests soccer. Football's only redeeming feature is that it was invented in England, but it began as a plebeian sport, with rough and rugged villagers kicking an inflated pig's bladder from one end of the country to the other, disrupting the hunting grounds of the old nobility. The dandy, meanwhile, sat in some aristocratic drawing-room, swapping gossip with duchesses and rising from his chair only to admire himself in a mirror.

Ronald Firbank, the dandy writer of the early twentieth century, didn't like football one bit. Vyvyan Holland once saw Firbank clad in a sweater and football shorts and asked him what on earth he had been doing. 'Oh, football,' replied Firbank. 'Rugger or soccer?' asked Holland. 'I don't remember,' said Firbank. 'Well,' Holland persisted, 'was the ball round or egg-shaped?' Firbank looked at him as if this was a ridiculous question to ask. 'I was never near enough to it to see that,' he said.

SEX

Thou shalt value pruience over prudery

If I speak of love in the context of dandyism, it is because love is the natural occupation of men of leisure.

CHARLES BAUDELAIRE

After my seventeenth glass of port, I suggested to my companion that we go a-wenching. He was, of course, amenable to the suggestion. I tried to disguise my baser instincts by wrapping them in a veil of poetic mystique, referring at the end of my rambling discourse to a remark made by Baudelaire.

'And so,' I concluded, 'love is the natural occupation of the man of leisure, the default setting of the dandy.'

'The dandy?' my companion exclaimed, sounding startled. 'What does the dandy have to do with wenches?'

'Whatever do you mean?' I asked.

'I thought,' he said, sounding somewhat edgy, 'that dandies weren't interested in girls. That they danced with the fairies, if you catch my drift.'

'And what makes you think that?'

'Oscar Wilde and those foppish chaps who hung around him – they were all at it, weren't they?'

'Forsooth!' I exclaimed. 'Neither prejudice nor prudery become you, sir.'

'I'm right, though, aren't I? Wilde went to prison for it. Sodomy, they called it at the time.'

'Which makes it sound so quaintly biblical, don't you think?' I asked.

'Bah!' said my companion, almost choking on his port.

'But, sir,' I continued, 'what you say is not without foundation. Wilde's ostentatious version of dandyism was seen as a homosexual phenomenon after his trial, and an obsession with fashion and the cult of high taste have subsequently become the widely-recognised characteristics of the gay stereotype.'

'Indeed!'

'And it is true,' I said, 'that some nineteenth century dandies were gay. Jean Lorrain, for example, was flamboyantly homosexual and delighted in an exaggerated exhibitionism realised through his own gaudy variant of dandyism.'

'Ha!' my companion proclaimed, as if vindicated.

'On the other hand,' I continued, 'many of the original dandies were heterosexual.'

'Name them!' he demanded.

'The greatest philosophers of dandyism, such as Baudelaire, Beerbohm and Barbey d'Aurevilly, were heterosexual,' I said, 'and many have been notorious womanisers – Casanova, Arthur Symons, and Théophile Gautier, for example. And let's not forget about James Bond.'

'So the great dandies were all straight?' my companion asked.

'No, no!' I replied. 'It's not that simple. Some were homosexual and some were heterosexual, and there is no connection at all between dandyism and sexual persuasion.'

'I accept your argument,' my friend said, 'but do so reluctantly.'

'Whether straight or gay,' I added, 'the dandy's sexual appetite will be prodigious. Casanova claimed to have seduced ten thousand women.'

'We've got some catching up to do!' said my companion. 'Let's find the fillies!'

And so, with our stomachs warmed by port, we embarked on a mission to corrupt the morals of London's most beautiful young girls. We sauntered off into the night, determined to contribute as best we could to the fall of this modern Babylon, and happy to have found at last our place in history.

RELIGION

Thou shalt be thine own religion

The sense of being perfectly well-dressed gives a feeling of inward tranquillity which religion is powerless to bestow.

RALPH WALDO EMERSON

Every creed promises a paradise which will be absolutely uninhabitable for anyone of civilised taste.

EVELYN WAUGH

People may say what they like about the decay of Christianity; the religious system that produced green Chartreuse can never really die.

SAKI

"What religion is the most stylish?' a friend asked, as if dipping a toe in the conversational water.

'I've heard that the fashion just now is a combination of Roman Catholic observance and atheistic attitudes,' I replied, admiring my fingernails. 'It's so clever. You get the antique splendour of the one and the modern convenience of the other.'

'Surely something as momentous as religion shouldn't be subject to the whims of fashion?'

'If fashion can dictate something as significant as the cut of a suit,' I replied, 'nothing is beyond its jurisdiction. Besides, religions are like dinner jackets. They have a certain degree of style regardless of the fine details.'

'I wouldn't say that myself,' he objected dryly. 'It all seems a bit inelegant to me. And dangerous to boot.'

'What?'

'One could so easily catch a chill by hanging around all day in a draughty church.'

'Health must be subordinate to style,' I said, taking a sip of my Campari soda. 'Any man can survive a bout of consumption if he remains stylish throughout, but good health alone cannot protect the man who suffers from a bout of vulgarity.'

'I think of all religion as being vulgar and inelegant,' my friend replied, 'what with all those clumsy ceremonies.'

'Clumsy? Surely not. Religious rituals gain charm through their utter perfection.'

'I prefer my rituals to be social,' he retorted. 'And besides, most garden parties involve more ceremony than a Latin mass.'

'Religious ceremony and ritual tend to reflect the ceremonies and rituals of society,' I theorised, 'for the religions of the world are simply reflections of the societies that created them.'

'In my opinion,' he proclaimed, puffing up his chest like a peacock, 'religion is, on the whole, fairly tasteless.'

'As a topic of conversation?' I jibed.

'No,' he said. 'In sartorial terms. Just think of the baggy

and shapeless frocks worn by those unfashionable priests.'

'Utter rot!' I retorted. 'Embroidered cassocks can be exquisite, in the right light. What religion are you, anyway?'

'I believe in nothing but myself,' he announced.

'If I was in your shoes,' I said, adjusting my tie, 'I think I would favour agnosticism.'

Chapter 3
THE HISTORY OF THE DANDY

Male splendour is a common characteristic in nature. The peacock struts his stuff, showing off his gaudy tail feathers both to state his dominance and to woo his female counterpart – the drab peahen who pales next to his glory. Such display has served the dandy in much the same way in human society – survival of the fitted, shall we say.

It has always been with us. The ancient Britons and the Celts loved nothing more than to daub their faces with woad and wield impressively shiny swords. The Anglo-Saxons delighted in ornate golden jewellery. Belt buckles and brooches were the most chic items in their wardrobes. King Alfred himself was a dandy of the first order. He was rather fond of jewellery, as is apparent from the Alfred Jewel, which the king inscribed with the words 'Alfred made me' so as to ensure that historians would credit him with good taste. During one rather famous incident, Alfred was too busy admiring his reflection on the back of a teaspoon to notice that the cakes were burning. The subsequent kings of England followed his lead and became more and more elaborate in their costumes. Henry VIII was renowned for his extravagant tastes. Gold lace frilled his jackets, and jewels were sewn into his clothes.

His daughter Elizabeth encouraged dandyism at her court. The chevaliers of the time of Queen Bess, like the Earl of Leicester, wore enormous ruffs and cultivated their pointy beards to delight and amuse their monarch. Unfortunately, however, the Elizabethan dandies, enamoured with the Renaissance ideal of virtuous action, were too busy dabbling in politics and war to loaf about doing nothing. They never had any spare time in which to nurture their nascent dandyism.

Dandyism declined in the reign of James I, a coarse and rugged Scotsman who disliked all the finer things in life. Charles I was too busy inciting civil war to care about his clothes. Oliver Cromwell and the Puritans of the Commonwealth denounced frippery and castigated those of a dandyish demeanour. This was a bleak period in the history of dandyism. The Restoration, however, saw the return of dandyism. Charles II, keen to show off the renewed strength of the Crown, dressed up in all his finery and paraded about town, the very picture of rejuvenated monarchical power. His courtiers were all dandies.

John Wilmot, the second Earl of Rochester, was a Restoration rake of the first order and a dandy of a raffish and disreputable nature. He began to hang out with the most caddish of Charles II's courtiers and spent all his money on vast quantities of wine, innumerable prostitutes, debauched living, and ostentatious extravagance. His depraved antics and riotous frolics were often the outcome of prolonged periods of drunkenness. Indeed, he claimed that he had maintained a steady state of utter intoxication for five consecutive years.

During this time, he set himself up as a quack doctor under the name of Alexander Bendo and amused himself by dispensing dubious advice and cosmetics to credulous women. A year or two later, he and the Duke of Buckingham rented a pub on the road to Newmarket. They posed as innkeepers with the aim of seducing every woman in the neighbourhood. He is remembered for his scurrilous satires, his sexually explicit verses, and his destructive alcoholism.

Sir George Etherege is said to have based the libertine Dorimant in his play of 1676, *The Man of Mode*, on Rochester. Another character in the play, Sir Fopling Flutter, an archetypal Restoration fop, was a portrait of Beau Hewit, the reigning exquisite of the hour. Like Rochester, Dorimant is a well-dressed womaniser. 'No man in town has a better fancy in his clothes than you have,' a friend tells him. Sir Fopling, on the other hand, 'thinks himself the pattern of modern gallantry' but is actually 'the pattern of modern foppery'. Medley dismisses Sir Fopling as effeminate: 'He was yesterday at the play, with a pair of gloves up to his elbows and a periwig more exactly curled than a lady's head newly dressed for a ball.' 'What a pretty lisp he has!' adds Young Bellair:

SIR FOPLING: A slight suit I made to appear in at my first arrival – not worthy your consideration, ladies.

DORIMANT:	The pantaloon is very well mounted.
SIR FOPLING:	The tassels are new and pretty.
MEDLEY:	I never saw a coat better cut.
SIR FOPLING:	It makes me show long waisted, and, I think, slender.
DORIMANT:	That's the shape our ladies dote on.
MEDLEY:	Your breech, though, is a handful too high, in my eye, Sir Fopling.
SIR FOPLING:	Peace, Medley, I have wished it lower a thousand times, but a pox on 't, 'twill not be!
LADY TOWNLEY:	His gloves are well fringed, large, and graceful.
SIR FOPLING:	I was always eminent for being *bien ganté.*

Over a century later, the first great dandy institution, the Macaroni Club, was founded in London. Named after its members' favourite dish, the club brought Continental fashions onto English dinner tables and into English wardrobes. The Macaronis were extravagant fops. Their 'uniform' – based on Italian fashions – featured very tight long-tailed coats, a trihorn hat, enormous white neck-cloths, pastel coloured breeches, white silk stockings, wigs a metre tall and high-heeled diamond-buckled red shoes. Jewellery, make-up and a bouquet of flowers (known as a 'nosegay') completed the look. For some time the moving spirit of the club was Charles James Fox, but the most fop-pish was Sir Lumley Skeffington, 'who used to paint his face, so that he looked like a French toy,' as one contemporary recorded. Excessively extravagant, foppish, ornate and bejewelled – this was the state of dandyism when a young man named Beau Brummell walked onto the boulevard of life and changed it for the better.

A member of the Macaroni Club

Chapter 4
BEAU BRUMMELL AND
THE REGENCY DANDIES

Dandyism as we know it was invented at the beginning of the nineteenth century. The Regency period – the last years of the reign of George III, when the Prince of Wales acted as Regent on account of his father's insanity – has come to be remembered for 'Regency style', a synthesis of the neo-classical and the exotic amidst the climax of literary and artistic Romanticism. The Regency age was also the mid-wife of English dandyism. In this period, one man attempt-ed to revolutionise men's fashions and create the philoso-phy of dandyism. His vision of the dandy was the product of his refined and unassuming perfection of dress. Though dandies had existed before, this man set the template for the dandy as we know him. For a short while his efforts bore fruit and the dandy cast in his image became a recog-nisable creature on the streets of London. Some, as you'll see, were more successful than others.

BEAU BRUMMELL

Brummell exerted such a powerful influence on men's appearance that the best of male sartorial fashions today are derived straight from his innovations.

Cecil Beaton

In certain congruities of dark cloth, in the rigid perfection of his linen, in the symmetry of his glove with his hand, lay the secret of Mr. Brummell's miracles … Mr. Brummell was, indeed, in the utmost sense of the word, an artist.

Max Beerbohm

Brummell saw nothing great but his tailor – nothing worthy of respect among the human arts but the art of cutting out a coat – and nothing fit to ensure human fame with posterity but the power to create and to bequeath a new fashion.

Blackwood's Edinburgh Magazine, June 1844

Take away the dandy and what remains of Brummell? He was fit for nothing more and for nothing less than to be the greatest dandy of his own or of any time … he was dandyism itself.

Jules Barbey d'Aurevilly

George Brummell, the ür-dandy, was born in 1778. When he left Oxford in 1794 at the age of sixteen, he took a commission in the Tenth Hussars, the most fashionable regiment of its day. The regiment was the Prince Regent's toy. Its only duty was to look splendid whilst accompanying the Prince on his pleasure-seeking travels. A place in the Hussars was a remarkable distinction, and as a result Brummell was introduced at once into the highest and most fashionable society.

Brummell's promotion was rapid, but he never really liked the army. A true dandy, he was too idle for anything that required any degree of regularity or discipline. He abhorred exertion of any sort, and he loved doing nothing. Things started to go wrong when he was required to wear hair powder at a time when it was ceasing to be fashionable. The final straw came when an order arrived stating that the regiment was to be quartered in a manufacturing town. Brummell rushed to see the Prince. 'The fact is, your Royal Highness, I have heard that we are ordered to Manchester,' said Brummell. 'Now, you must be aware how disagreeable this would be to me. I really could not go. Think! Manchester!' As a result, Brummell left the army in 1798, stripping himself of the highest opportunity in the showiest of all professions before he was twenty-one.

He moved to a house in Chesterfield Street in Mayfair. There he gave small but exquisite dinners to which he invited men of rank – including the Prince himself – to his table. He was immediately made a member of White's, the most exclusive gentleman's club of the era. He spent his days sitting in the famous bow window there, criticising the clothes of the people walking past on the street outside. He was once asked why he was there without fail on rainy days. 'I like to see the dem'd people getting wet,' he replied.

Brummell became well known for his style and perfection in dress and for many years was regarded by high society as the ultimate authority on all matters of dress. His costume was impeccable and finished with perfect skill, but without exaggeration. He avoided elaborate clothes, and would never be seen wearing fantastic colours, lace, jewels or perfumes.

The Beau claimed that 'the severest mortification which a gentleman could incur was to attract observation in the street by his outward appearance,' but Brummell did always attract observation by his outward appearance. People stared when he walked by, scrutinising his perfection, taking note of the height of his cape or the cut of his jacket, and scurrying home to adapt their clothes to match his.

His morning dress comprised beige buckskins and a blue coat with brass buttons, the coat tails ending at the knee and the lapels rising to the ears. Under the coat he wore a buff-coloured waistcoat buttoned incredibly tight so as to produce a small waist, and opening at the breast to expose a frilled shirt and cravat. He wore shiny black boots, of which even the soles were highly polished. Brummell's style was in fact simplicity, but simplicity of the most studied kind.

Unlike most men of his era, Brummell was keen on cleanliness. He didn't usually emerge from his dressing room until mid-afternoon and spent at least two hours a day on his appearance. His regime was endowed with the precision of ritual. He brushed his teeth, shaved with extreme care, washed and scrubbed with hot water, and exfoliated with a stiff pigskin-bristle brush. He was proud of his personal hygiene, and avoided perfumes not because he disliked them but because he didn't need them. 'No perfumes,' he used to say, 'but fine linen, plenty of it, and country washing.' He objected to rural squires being introduced to his club on the ground that they always smelt of horse-dung.

As a leader of fashion, Brummell acquired social power. With the awareness of this power came his infamous effrontery and impertinence. He soon came to be as famous for his truculent wit and blasé demeanour as he was for his style. The Duke of Bedford once asked Brummell his opinion of a new coat. 'Turn around,' said the Beau. Feeling the lapel delicately with his thumb, Brummell asked in his most piteous manner, 'Bedford, do you call this thing a coat?' Brummell's impertinence led to a vitriolic quarrel with the Prince Regent. Brummell, keen to have the butler bring refreshments, turned to the Prince and said, 'Ring the bell, George'. The Prince, as angry with Brummell's superior tone of voice as he was at the use of his first name, ordered him to leave immediately.

After his famous quarrel with the Prince Regent, Brummell was walking down St. James's Street with Lord Moira when they saw the Prince approaching. The Prince stopped and spoke to Lord Moira but ignored Brummell.

As soon as he turned away, Brummell asked Lord Moira in a loud voice, 'Pray, who is your fat friend?'

Brummell's inheritance amounted to £30,000, but he was a reckless gambler and was soon ruined. He built up enormous debts and fled to the Continent in 1816 to escape his creditors. Byron's friend Lord Broughton said that this was 'as great a fall as Napoleon's.' It was certainly dramatic. On the evening of his planned escape, Brummell dined at his club and went to the opera. During the interval he slipped into the shadows and met a four-horse carriage to take him to Dover. His creditors, however, had been keeping an eye on him, and they followed in hot pursuit. But Brummell had gained the advantage of a head start, and he travelled all night. He reached Dover by morning, climbed aboard a boat, and left England and his creditors behind. As debtors could not be followed to France, Brummell was secure.

Brummell lived in Calais for nearly the rest of his life. For a man accustomed to the highest luxuries of London life, this was a rude awakening and may have contributed to his decline. He was imprisoned briefly for debt in France and died in 1840, aged sixty-two, in a mental institution – a filthy, ragged and incontinent man, incapable of speech and entirely unrecognisable as the great Beau who had once ruled London society. This was a sorry end, but his death barely rippled the social pond back in England.

Brummell was no mere fop. In his own subtle way, he inaugurated a social revolution. This man, the son of a commoner, created a new aristocracy – an aristocracy based not on inherited wealth and title, but on style and sophistication. His sense of superiority was clear from his aplomb, his sheer nerve and unconquerable self-assurance. 'You seem to have caught cold, Brummell,' a friend once said on hearing him cough. 'Yes,' replied Brummell. 'A wretch of an innkeeper put me into the coffee-room with a damp stranger.' By becoming the supreme dictator in matters of dress, he became more important than royalty. Indeed, the Prince Regent is said to have wept when Brummell disapproved of the cut of the royal coat.

Beau Brummell

THE PRINCE REGENT

I try and take him to pieces, and find silk stockings, paddings, stays, a coat with frogs and a fur collar, a star and blue ribbon, a pocket-handkerchief prodigiously scented, one of Truefitt's best nutty-brown wigs reeking with oil, a set of teeth and a huge black stock, underwaistcoats, more underwaistcoats, and then nothing.

William Makepeace Thackeray on the Prince Regent

George was born in London on 12th August 1762. As the Prince of Wales, he became notorious for his dandyism, wild behaviour and appalling extravagance. His love affairs became the scandal of his generation. After a fling with a young actress named Perdita, he acquired several mistresses before secretly marrying a Roman Catholic, Mrs Fitzherbert, in 1785. Less than two years later, to obtain money for his debts, he asked Parliament to declare the marriage illegal.

His second marriage, ten years later, was to his cousin, a German hippopotamus of a girl named Princess Caroline of Brunswick. The first time he clapped eyes on her, a few days before the wedding was due to take place, he turned to his aide and said, 'Harris, I am not well. Pray get me a glass of brandy'. He needed to marry, however, in order to liquidate his debts, and so the planned ceremony went ahead. Brummell nicknamed the portly pair 'Big Ben and Benita'. It came as no surprise when he split up with fat Caroline after the birth of their daughter, Princess Charlotte, in 1796. Caroline detested George so much that she had taken to sticking pins into wax images of him that she then placed by the fire.

George became Prince Regent in 1811, when his father became mentally unable to discharge his duties, and at this point his extravagant foppery reached new heights. A contemporary remembered his clothes: 'His coat was pink silk, with white cuffs; his waistcoat was white silk, embroidered with various coloured foil.' Brummell tried to educate the Prince in the matter of simple and elegant style, and for a while his teaching bore fruit as the Prince aped Brummell's refined and modest perfection of dress.

After their famous argument, however, the Prince abandoned Brummell's advice and returned to his former ways. After his death, his entire wardrobe was sold at auction and realised £15,000, although it was reckoned that the original cost of his clothes was nearer to £100,000. A list of the sale items was published with the comment: 'Wealth has done wonders, taste not much.' Eighteen years without Brummell had not done him any good at all.

LORD ALVANLEY

William Arderne, the second Baron Alvanley, was a friend of the Prince Regent and one of the more unusual members of the Prince's circle. He was also one of the most prominent Regency bucks, and as a dandy almost rivalled Beau Brummell himself. Indeed, upon Brummell's disgrace and ruin, Lord Alvanley came to be regarded as leader of the dandies and 'first gentleman in England'.

Alvanley's riotous dinner parties were famous. There were never more than eight guests present, and apricot tart was invariably thrown around the room. His guests were alarmed by his habit of extinguishing candles by flinging them on the floor or smothering them with bedsheets. Alvanley was a generous and witty friend, but a fearsome enemy. He had a bad temper and was notorious for his readiness to fight duels with anyone who annoyed him. He once fought a duel on Wimbledon Common with Morgan O'Connell, who, in the House of Commons, had called him a 'bloated buffoon'.

Alvanley was a member of White's and Watier's clubs, where he gambled recklessly. His enormous gambling debts and his great extravagance led to the break-up of the family estates. The family lost Underbank Hall – it was sold by auction in 1823 – and two years later the Bredbury estate had to be sold after Alvanley unwisely purchased some rather expensive snuffboxes.

POODLE BYNG

The Regency dandy Frederick Gerald Byng, the fifth son of Viscount Torrington, was known as 'Poodle' Byng to his friends. He was fond of letting his light hair curl around his forehead, and his pet poodle accompanied him wherever he went. One day he was driving in his coach with his poodle at his side when Brummell called out, 'Ah, how do you do, Byng? A family vehicle, I see.'

As a Gentleman Usher of the Royal Chamber, Poodle Byng was appointed by the Foreign Minister to escort the Hawaiian royal family during an unexpected visit to London in 1824. Byng's role as a chaperone was made rather easy by the fact that the unfortunate King Kamehameha II and Queen Tamehamalu died at Osborne's Hotel in July of measles and inflammation of the lungs.

Byng was one of the group who sat with Beau Brummell in the bow window at White's judging the dress of passers-by. He married Catherine Neville, his mother's maid, and towards the end of his life he was known as a 'Regency Remnant'. He was unusual amongst the Regency dandies: he never once felt it necessary to flee the country.

ROMEO COATES

The Regency dandy Robert 'Romeo' Coates inherited a large fortune and an enormous collection of diamonds from his father, a sugar planter who had made his fortune in the West Indies. Coates put diamond buttons on his jackets, diamond buckles on his shoes, and sprinkled diamonds on his elaborate wigs. His passion in life was theatre, and he loved Shakespeare. After experimenting with amateur dramatics, he turned professional and persuaded the manager of a theatre in Bath to let him play Romeo on stage – hence his nickname. Posters announced that 'a Gentleman of Fashion' would star in Romeo and Juliet and tickets sold like hot cakes.

On the evening of the first performance, Coates got a bit carried away. He burst onto the stage wearing scarlet tights, a sky-blue cloak, a Charles II wig, a top hat, an enormous cravat, masses of real diamonds and a grin like a manic simpleton. He improvised disastrously. In the balcony scene he produced a large snuffbox, took a pinch himself and asked the bewildered Juliet if she would like some. His death scene was so utterly ludicrous that the gallery called for an encore.

Humiliated, he fled to London where, unable to suppress his desire for an audience, he became one of the main tourist attractions, driving around in an ornate carriage shaped like a kettledrum, drawn by a team of pure white horses. A large golden cockerel was stuck on the side of this carriage, underneath which was painted Romeo's new motto – 'While I live I'll crow'.

Frederick 'Poodle' Byng

GOLDEN BALL HUGHES

Edward Hughes Ball assumed the surname Hughes in 1819 after an Uncle on his mother's side who left him a fortune of £40,000 a year. He then became Edward Hughes Ball Hughes, but he was known to his friends as 'Golden Ball' due to his wealth and flamboyance. He was dedicated to following fashionable pursuits. He kept a large stable of hunters, but he seldom rode. He kept a box at Covent Garden, but disliked the theatre. He kept a box at His Majesty's Theatre, but he was bored by the Opera. He shot partridges, but not for long, and most escaped his gun. As Saki put it, there's a deadly sameness about partridges; when you've missed one, you've missed the lot.

Golden Ball was celebrated for his chocolate coloured coach and for his invention of the black cravat, but he became notorious as a result of events one evening in 1823. The King's Theatre was packed with an audience eager to see a beautiful sixteen-year-old Spanish dancer, Maria Mercandotti, who was the toast of London. The manager, however, appeared and expressed his regret that Mercandotti had disappeared. Subsequently it transpired that she had eloped with Golden Ball Hughes. Harrison Ainsworth, the novelist, summed up the matter very neatly:

The fair damsel has gone; and no wonder at all,
That bred to the dance she is gone to the Ball.

Hughes bought Oatlands from the Duke of York in 1820 after the death of the Duchess of York. He then squandered his inheritance, sold Oatlands to pay his debts, fled to Paris to escape his creditors and died in poverty. The root of all evil is not so much the love of money as the burning desire to get rid of it. Without evil, however, there can be no good. Spend, spend, spend!

RED HERRINGS HERTFORD

The Marquess of Hertford was a Regency rake known as 'Red Herrings' to his friends, a nickname derived in part from his red hair and in part from his tendency to make utterly irrelevant remarks in conversation. A friend of the Prince Regent, Hertford was also a hedonist and a voluptuary who made a habit of seducing married women.

One of his contemporaries described him as 'a man without one redeeming quality in the multitude of his glaring, damning vices … the debauched sensualist, the heartless roué, the gamester.' This judgement was perhaps a little too harsh. Hertford, it seems, was a well-educated, highly civilised and exquisitely cultured man. Harriette Wilson, one of Hertford's many mistresses, described him in glowing terms:

> He is a man possessing more general knowledge than anyone I know. His Lordship appears to be *au fait* on every subject one can possibly imagine. Talk to him of drawing, or horse-riding; painting or cock-fighting; rhyming, cooking or fencing; profligacy or morals; religion of whatever creed; languages living or dead; claret, or burgundy; furnishing houses or breeding parrots; and you might see that he had served his apprenticeship to every one of them.

And with Hertford's tendency towards irrelevant remarks,

one can well imagine that he would have been able to flit through all these subjects in a five-minute chat.

LORD PETERSHAM

Princess Lieven, the wife of the Russian ambassador, called Petersham 'the maddest of all the mad Englishmen'. Petersham certainly was a little mad, but he proved that eccentricity could be fashionable. At the age of fifteen he joined the Coldstream Guards as an ensign and became a military dandy. He attained the rank of lieutenant colonel whilst in his thirties, but suddenly decided to retire in 1812 in order to devote his life to the serious pursuit of pleasure. He lived in London and became a leader of fashion, introducing the ridiculously wide 'Cossack' trousers made of garish striped material but with excessively narrow waists and ankles.

Petersham was a genuine eccentric who dressed and behaved in a peculiar manner simply because he felt like it. When he fell in love with a widow named Mary Browne, he decided that everything in his life should be a particular shade of brown in tribute to his unrequited love. He bought a brown carriage, brown horses, brown harnesses and brown livery for his servants. From his tailor he ordered a brown silk coat embroidered with dead leaves. As Princess Lieven wrote to Meternich, 'You can see what kind of man he is.' Petersham's subsequent affair with Lady Francis Webster caused a great deal of gossip, particularly after her husband tried to horsewhip him in the middle of St James's.

SCROPE DAVIES

Scrope's manners and appearance were of the true Brummell type: there was nothing showy in his exterior. He was quiet and reserved in ordinary company, but he was the life and soul of those who relished learning and wit.

Captain Gronow

Scrope Davies, a friend of Byron and Brummell, was a dandy, a womaniser, a drinker and a reckless gambler. Byron records that in 1808 they left Scrope at a gambling house one night at midnight when he was drunk, penniless and refusing to go home. The next day, with empty pockets and severe headaches, they went to his house at two o'clock in the afternoon. There they found him sound asleep next to a chamber pot brim-full of banknotes. When he awoke he could not remember how he had obtained this small fortune. Davies lived extravagantly, squandered his inheritance and amassed enormous debts. In 1820, he was – needless to say – forced to flee England to escape creditors.

LORD BYRON

Perhaps, had Byron not been a dandy – but ah, had he not been in his soul a dandy there would have been no Byron worth mentioning. And it was because he guarded not his dandyism against this and that irrelevant passion, sexual or political, that he cut so annoyingly incomplete a figure.

Max Beerbohm

The truth is that though I gave up the business early I had a tinge of dandyism in my minority, and probably retained enough of it to conciliate the great ones; at four and twenty I had gamed, and drank, and taken my degrees in most dissipations; and having no pedantry, and not being overbearing, we ran quietly together. I knew them all more or less, and they made me a Member of Watier's (a superb Club at that time), being, I take it, the only literary man in it.

George Byron

Born in London in 1788, the poet George Byron was the son of Captain 'Mad Jack' Byron and the grandson of Admiral 'Foulweather Jack' Byron. Lame from birth, George grew up in Aberdeen at his mother's shabby lodgings. In 1798, on the death of 'the wicked lord', his great-uncle, George Byron became the sixth Baron Byron of Rochdale.

In 1805 he went to Trinity in Cambridge, where he led a dissipated and rebellious life. An early collection of his poems was published as *Hours of Idleness* in acknowledgement of his tendency towards lethargy. Whilst at college, Byron decided that he wanted to keep a dog. He was told that this was against the college's rules, so he bought a bear instead. He kept it in the small hexagonal tower above his rooms, and he enjoyed the sensation he made when he took it for walks on a leash. After university, he set out on a grand tour, visiting Spain, Malta, Albania, Greece and the Aegean. He developed a love of Albanian costumes, which were, he said, 'as fine as pheasants'. He eventually bought some magnificent Albanian costumes, embroidered with gold, which he got for a snip at fifty guineas each.

On his return, he became the darling of London society and the lover of Lady Caroline Lamb. He frequented all the fashionable clubs and drank with the leading lights of the fashionable world. He was on good terms with Brummell, who he praised as having 'a certain exquisite propriety of dress'. 'I liked the dandies,' Byron wrote in 1822, 'they were always very civil to me.' Byron later claimed that there were only three great men of his age: himself, Napoleon and Brummell.

Byron always liked to cause a stir. When his gardener brought him a human skull that had been unearthed, Byron had it made into a drinking cup by a jeweller. The event was worthy of a poem, entitled 'Lines Inscribed upon a Cup Formed from a Skull'.

And as only a true dandy can, Byron influenced the

world of fashion for a short time. Young men throughout England imitated his look with varying degrees of success, and every fashionable man worth his salt tried his best to look ill and unhappy. Nonchalance was the only facial expression in vogue. Instead of a smile and a cheery saluta-tion, people greeted one another with a deep and fatal look in the eyes and lips showing scorn towards humanity.

Perhaps the best pen-portrait of Byron is by his one-time friend John Polidori, a talented individual who com-mitted suicide at the age of twenty-six because of crippling gambling debts. Polidori, who had travelled on the Continent with Byron, used Byron as the model for his dandy vampire, Lord Ruthven, in his famous tale of 1819, *The Vampyre*:

> There appeared at the various parties the *ton* of a noble-man, more remarkable for his singularities, than his rank... His peculiarities caused him to be invited to every house; all wished to see him, and those who had been accustomed to violent excitement, and now felt the weight of *ennui*, were pleased to have something in their presence capable of engaging their attention.

Ruthven has the 'reputation of a winning tongue' and 'irresistible powers of seduction'. He specialises in corrupt-ing innocent young women and taking their blood to pro-long his own existence. The analogy between the dandy and the vampire is appropriate on a scale far wider than that of the simple Byron-Ruthven matrix. The vampire, like the dandy, has elegant manners, impeccable dress and an aristocratic bearing. Both these artificial creatures of the night are epic seducers of women. The analogy must not be carried too far. To my knowledge, no real-life dandy has ever taken a liking to blood. The very idea! Bloodstains can ruin a good shirt, you know.

Chapter 5
ENGLISH DANDIES
FROM 1820 TO 1850

When Brummell fell, the Brummellian version of the dandy fell too. His modest perfection of dress was superseded by a new fashion. Reacting against Brummell's refined simplicity, the dandies developed an excessive flamboyancy. Lace and frills became chic again. Bright colours were everywhere to be seen. If Brummell was a sight for sore eyes, the post-Brummell dandy, striving to be more ludicrous than the next man, was a sight capable of making one's eyes feel decidedly sore.

COUNT D'ORSAY

He is the divinity of dandies. In another age he would have passed into the court of the gods, and youths would have sacrificed to the God of fashion.

CHARLES SUMNER

Count D'Orsay, whose name is publicly synonymous with elegant and graceful accomplishment, and who, by those who knew him well, is affectionately remembered and regretted, as a man whose great abilities might have raised him to any distinction, and whose gentle heart even a world of fashion left unspoiled.

CHARLES DICKENS

As the *arbiter elegantiarum*, he has reigned supreme in matters of taste and fashion, confirming the attempts of others by his approbation, or gratifying them by his example.

NEW MONTHLY MAGAZINE, 1845

Alfred Guillame Gabriel D'Orsay was by title a Count of France, and he hailed from a rich provincial family. In England, however, he frequently found himself running short of cash and was supported by the generosity of Lord and Lady Blessington who gave D'Orsay everything he needed.

Lord Blessington died in 1829, and by his will made D'Orsay his executor and major heir. To qualify for the Blessington fortune, however, D'Orsay had to marry one of Blessington's young daughters. He married the fifteen-year-old Lady Harriet on condition that he would refrain from consummating the marriage until she reached the age of twenty — a condition imposed by the jealous Lady Blessington who wanted D'Orsay for herself. At the age of nineteen, however, Lady Harriet ran away from D'Orsay and hid at the house of some benevolent relatives. D'Orsay, it seems, had sought to persuade Lady Harriet to consummate the marriage earlier than allowed.

D'Orsay seemed not to mind that his wife had left him. He spent his time at Crockford's, the late Regency gambling club, which was by then the most fashionable club in London. He reigned supreme as London's arch-dandy and the supreme arbiter in matters of taste and fashion. His looks were striking. A tall and imposing man, he wore his bright auburn hair in a mass of glossy ringlets. His clothes were of pastel velvets and silks, embellished with gold buttons, topped with a satin cravat and an extravagantly tall hat.

The splendour of his flashy clothes was hard to miss, but it was the splendour of his personality that impressed those who met him. They spoke highly of his amiability, his firm handshake and infectious laugh, his imperturbable self-confidence, and his perpetual high spirits. Disraeli dedicated his 1833 novel *Godolphin* to D'Orsay, and in 1836 he immortalised D'Orsay in print in *Henrietta Temple* as

'Count Alcibiades de Mirabel'. Dickens gave D'Orsay the honour of being godfather to his sixth child. In 1852, when Prince Louis Napoleon became Napoleon III, the new Emperor appointed D'Orsay as the Director of Fine Arts for the Second Empire. This crowning glory to his career as a dandy was not to last long. D'Orsay died a few days after hearing of his new appointment, remembered by everyone not as a Count of France, nor as a Director of Fine Arts, but as the God of Fashion.

Count D'Orsay

EDWARD BULWER LYTTON

Names are of the utmost importance to dandies. Beau Brummell never mentioned the fact that his middle name was Bryan. Thomas Wainewright wrote under the pseudonyms Egomet Bonmot and Cornelius Van Vinckbooms. After his release from prison, Oscar Wilde changed his name to Sebastian Melmoth. The dandy author and politician Edward Bulwer Lytton may have felt the need for a pseudonym, for his full name was a real tongue twister – Sir Edward George Earle Lytton Bulwer Bulwer Lytton. Thackeray mocked him for it, dubbing him 'Sawedwadgeorgearllittnbulwig'.

As a result of juvenile name-based japes and other such tomfoolery, Bulwer disliked other children and refused to go to Eton. Instead he was taught at home by a private tutor in London where he was educated in the ways of society. He attended innumerable dinners and balls, and soon got bored by it all. 'At the age of twenty-two,' he wrote, 'I hated balls as much as they are hated by most men of twenty-five.' Despite this severe *ennui*, he continued to figure prominently in British and Continental social circles, which were intimately described in his second novel, *Pelham*, which was published in 1828.

A French reviewer praised *Pelham* as 'the most pure and most perfect manual of dandyism'. Subtitled *The Adventures of a Gentleman*, the book tells the story of 'the making of a man by means of dandyism'. Pelham's dandyism is a pose

– a meticulous, conscious and effective pose. 'Careless and indifferent as I seem to all things,' says Pelham, 'nothing ever escapes me: the minutest *erreur* in a dish or a domestic, the most trifling peculiarity in a criticism or a coat, my glance detects in an instant, and transmits for ever to my recollection.' Pelham lives his life by his maxim: 'Manage yourself well, and you may manage all the world.'

Pelham was criticised by Thomas Carlyle in *Sartor Resartus*. In Chapter 10 of Book 3, Carlyle ridiculed Bulwer's views on dress by parodying them as 'Articles of Faith'. 'The good sense of a gentleman,' mocked Carlyle, 'is nowhere more finely developed than in his rings.' Carlyle also claimed that he suffered from delirium tremens whenever he tried to read a fashionable novel. He stopped reading such books, he said, 'by order of the doctor, dreading ruin to my whole intellectual and bodily facilities.' Bulwer reacted to this criticism. The first edition of *Pelham* had contained an entire chapter on the subject of dress. For subsequent editions, however, Bulwer edited out this chapter, and since 1836 *Pelham* has never been reprinted in its original unedited version.

Despite Carlyle's vitriol, *Pelham* set a new fashion. As a result of Bulwer's views on dress, black and white became the new fashion for men's evening wear. Beau Brummell, in self-imposed exile by this time, disapproved of this trend. Brummell's biographer, Captain Jesse, arrived at Brummell's house in Calais wearing this newly fashionable evening costume of black and white. 'My dear Jesse,' said Brummell, who wore blue, 'I am sadly afraid you have been reading *Pelham*. Excuse me, but you look very much like a magpie.'

Bulwer was an archetypal 'butterfly dandy' with a head of beautiful curls and an extravagant dress sense. In a 1841 piece for *Fraser's Magazine* called 'Men and Coats', Thackeray blamed the defects of Bulwer's literary style on his dandyism: 'a certain popular writer is in the habit of composing his works in a large-flowered damask dressing gown, and morocco slippers,' he jeered.

Bulwer was annoyed by this ridicule and scorn. As soon as people stopped laughing at his name, they started sniggering at his clothes. He toned down his image when he went into politics, but he was always the best-dressed man in the Palace of Westminster. 'I suppose Bulwer is making money,' wrote Macaulay, 'for his coat must cost as much as that of any five other members of parliament.'

PENDENNIS

William Makepeace Thackeray may have mocked Bulwer, but he saw fit to create his own fictional dandy. Thackeray's *History of Pendennis* (1848) is the tale of a young man making his way in the world, adopting and perfecting dandyism. Pendennis enters a small but fashionable college in 'the University of Oxbridge' and becomes a consummate dandy. 'Pen, during his time at university,' Thackeray tells us, 'was rather a dressy man, and loved to array himself in splendour.'

He dresses in the post-Brummell style, 'appearing in the morning in wonderful shooting-jackets, with remarkable buttons; and in the evening in gorgeous velvet waistcoats, with richly embroidered cravats.' Pen becomes a gambler and a hedonist: 'Pen's appetite for pleasure was insatiable, and he rushed at it wherever it presented itself, with an eagerness which bespoke his fiery constitution and youthful health. He called taking pleasure "seeing life".'

Soon he is regarded as 'a young buck' and in the course of his second year he becomes 'one of the men of fashion' in the university:

> He and his polite friends would dress themselves out with as much care in order to go and dine at each other's rooms, as other folks would who were going to enslave a mistress. They said he used to wear rings over his kid gloves, which he always denies … That he took per-

fumed baths is a truth; and he used to say that he took them after meeting certain men of a very low set in hall.

Edward Bulwer Lytton

BENJAMIN DISRAELI

'A smile for a friend, and a sneer for the world, is the way to govern mankind,' wrote Disraeli in his first novel *Vivian Grey*. As a young man with social aspirations and a desire to govern mankind, Disraeli developed his dandyism as a sneer at the world. It was an isolated pedestal of self on which he stood and drew attention to himself, relishing his sense of being different.

Disraeli was born into a Jewish home but was baptised at thirteen. He went to a small provincial school and left at the age of sixteen. He did not go to university. Instead he spent a year at home and picked up his education under the guidance of his father, Isaac D'Israeli, a literary scholar. The young Disraeli was faced with two problems: he was both an unknown and an outsider. If he remained either, his burning desire to govern mankind could not be realised. Dandyism, he decided, was the only solution.

In 1821 he was articled to a firm of solicitors. One of the partners remembered his 'rather conspicuous attire' – a black velvet suit, black stockings and bright red shoes. Edward Bulwer Lytton recalled seeing Disraeli in green velvet trousers, a yellow waistcoat, a shirt frilled with lace and silver buckles on his shoes. When he travelled to Turkey, young Dizzy became even more ostentatious. 'You should see me in the costume of a Greek pirate,' he wrote home. 'A blood-red shirt, with silver studs as big as shillings, an immense scarf for a girdle, full of pistols and daggers, red cap, red slippers, broad blue striped jacket and trousers'.

Disraeli's dandyism certainly won him the attention he craved. No one could fail to notice this dashing young man attired in a purple trousers with a gold band down the seam, a black velvet coat and a scarlet waistcoat, with lace ruffles falling to the tips of his fingers, shimmering with a profusion of jewels and chains.

Vivian Grey was published in 1826. Vivian, the central character, is 'an elegant, lively lad, with just enough of dandyism to preserve him from committing gaucheries, and with a devil of a tongue'. The early editions of the novel contained a whole chapter on dress, which Disraeli cut out of later editions, embarrassed, like Bulwer, by the excesses of his youth. Another early novel, *The Young Duke*, tells of the adventures of a young aristocratic dandy whose elegance, like his vanity, knows no bounds.

Having gained attention, Disraeli became friends with Bulwer and, thanks to his efforts, entered into society in 1831. Bulwer invited Disraeli to dinner parties, and it was at these parties that Disraeli met Mrs Wyndham Lewis, his future wife, whose family connections helped to get Disraeli a seat in Parliament, and Count D'Orsay, the great Parisian dandy, whose family connections got Disraeli into Crockford's and Almack's, the most exclusive clubs of the day.

Disraeli, like Bulwer, toned down his garish dandyism of dress in order to enter the world of politics, but he always retained a certain dandyism of manner. As a man of relentless personal ambition, Disraeli climbed to the top of the greasy pole, but power came to him late. He became Prime Minister in 1868 and again, at the age of seventy, in 1874.

If the young Disraeli wished to be Vivian Grey, the old Disraeli saw himself as the character Sidonia in his novel *Coningsby* — an outsider, a man of almost pure intellect, blessed with 'that absolute freedom from prejudice, which was the compensating possession of a man without a country'. The special perception of the outsider became his passport to being accepted as an insider, serving the same purpose as his youthful dandyism. By drawing attention to himself, and by glorifying his sense of being different, he was at first noticed and then accepted by the world to which he wished to belong. John Bright summed it up when he remarked that Disraeli was a self-made man who worshipped his creator.

THOMAS WAINEWRIGHT

Thomas Griffiths Wainewright, born in 1794, was brought up first by his grandfather, a maverick of the literary world who had made his fortune by publishing *Fanny Hill*. After his grandfather died of natural causes, Wainewright went to live with an uncle, who soon died of unnatural causes, poisoned by Wainewright. The poisoner inherited his uncle's elegant London house as a result, but he lacked the means to live there in the manner to which he aspired. After a brief period in the army he became art critic of *London Magazine*.

This was the most exciting literary magazine of the age. Charles Lamb was the essayist-in-residence, William Hazlitt the drama critic. De Quincey's *Confessions of an English Opium Eater* and John Clare's early poems were first published within its pages. Wainewright wrote for his magazine under the pseudonyms Egomet Bonmot, Janus Weathercock and Cornelius Van Vinckbooms. The publishers held brilliant dinner parties, which Wainewright attended wearing beautiful rings over his pale lemon-coloured kid gloves. Within a short time he had established a reputation as both a dandy and a wit. 'Like Disraeli,' wrote Oscar Wilde in his essay on Wainewright, 'he determined to startle the town as a dandy ... There was something in him of Balzac's Lucien de Rubempré.'

Wilde regarded Wainewright as the precursor of such aesthetes as Walter Pater. 'He was one of the first to recognise … the very keynote of aesthetic eclecticism,' argued Wilde, 'the true harmony of all really beautiful things irrespective of age or place, of school or manner.' Wilde also looked upon Wainewright as the forefather of his own dandyism. 'This young dandy,' wrote Wilde, 'sought to be somebody, rather than to do something. He recognised that Life itself is an art.'

As an aesthete and connoisseur, the dandy wishes to live lavishly and to surround himself with beautiful objects. To do so, he needs a substantial income. Here Wainewright was thwarted. He was too poor to play the part of the man-about-town, so this arch-schemer came up with a plan. In the course of 1830, he persuaded his sister-in-law, a pretty young woman called Helen Abercrombie, to take out life insurance policies with five different companies. Her life was then worth the very considerable sum of £18,000.

Within days of filling out the paperwork and drawing up a new will in favour of Wainewright, Helen was discovered vomiting and blind. Her pulse was racing, but soon she was dead. The autopsy report suggested a cerebral haemorrhage, but the balance of evidence suggests that Wainewright had fed her jelly laced with strychnine. It seems that the suspicious death of his mother-in-law may also have been his work.

Although there was nothing to prove that he was a murderer, Wainewright was uneasy about spending his ill-gotten gains in London. He moved to Paris, where he created for himself a life of luxurious leisure. After a few years, he returned to England and was arrested in connection with another crime, a small matter of fraud. He was found guilty of forging a legal document and sentenced to transportation for life. In the penal colony in Australia, he established himself as a successful studio artist.

Although he was never actually brought to trial for murder, Wainewright was happy to admit that he was a murderer. When accused to his face of the murder of Helen Abercrombie, he did not deny it. 'It was a dreadful thing to do,' he said, shrugging his shoulders, 'but she had very thick ankles.' His exploits inspired a best-selling novel by Bulwer Lytton and a short story by Dickens. 'To be suggestive for fiction,' Wilde concludes, 'is to be of more importance than a fact.'

Benjamin Disreali

CHARLES DICKENS

Dandyism? There is no King George the Fourth now
(more the pity) to set the dandy fashion; there are no
clear-starched jack-towel neckcloths, no short-waisted
coats, no false calves, no stays. There are no caricatures,
now, of effeminate exquisites so arrayed, swooning in
opera boxes with excess of delight and being revived by
other dainty creatures poking long-necked scent-bottles
at their noses. There is no beau whom it takes four
men at once to shake into his buckskins, or who is
troubled with the self-reproach of having once consumed a pea.

CHARLES DICKENS, *Bleak House*

When Dickens's wife Catherine gave birth to their sixth
child, Dickens asked his friend and mentor Count D'Orsay
to act as godfather. The other godfather was Tennyson, and
the unlucky boy was christened Alfred D'Orsay Tennyson
Dickens. Edward Fitzgerald thought that the name reeked
of 'Snobbishness and Cockneyism'. Fitzgerald's charming
remark encapsulates the essence of Dickens's dandyism. As
a writer he may have been a tremendous success, but as a
dandy he was a failure.

His rise to fame had been meteoric. *Sketches by Boz*
appeared in 1836 when Dickens was only twenty-four and
The Pickwick Papers followed in 1837, with *Oliver Twist*
cementing his position as a star in the literary firmament in

1838. In his mid-twenties, as his literary stature grew, Dickens tried to become a dandy. He met D'Orsay and Bulwer and admired them. He became a follower of the D'Orsay style.

He bought a new hat and a blue cloak, clothes of brilliant colours, a swallowtail coat with a high velvet collar, a crimson velvet waistcoat, long gold watch-chain, and Cossack trousers. For evening-wear, he sported black pantaloons with buttons at the ankles, a frilly shirt and a white cravat ornamented with a bow eight inches wide. This was all topped off with a striking mop of curly brown hair. Ostentatious dress was the hallmark of Dickens the Dandy, and Dickens himself admitted that he had 'the fondness of a savage for finery'.

The aristocracy sneered at Dickens's vulgarity. His clothes were too extravagant to be stylish. His early novels were not fashionable. He wrote stories about the poor and the middle classes which sold in serial form – 'a low, cheap form of publication' – instead of appearing as slim, leather-bound volumes. And – if more proof were needed to demonstrate Dickens's lack of taste – these novels sold in huge numbers to the malodorous masses.

Dickens retaliated by striking out against his detractors and their aristocratic dandyism. In Chapter 12 of *Bleak House* he complained about aristocratic dandies who had 'agreed to put a smooth glaze on the world and to keep down all its realities. For whom everything must be languid and pretty ... Who are to rejoice at nothing and be sorry for nothing. Who are not to be disturbed by ideas.' His tirade was personal, and he railed against 'dandyism of a more mischievous sort, that has got below the surface,' by which he meant the aristocratic tendency to sneer at the vulgar.

But Dickens was not cowed. He persisted in his dandyism. As he got older, despite the fact that his features broadened, coarsened and reddened from over-eating, his dress sense became even more theatrical. By 1870, Dickens became aware that the public persona he had created for himself was becoming ludicrous. In *Our Mutual Friend*, he places his thoughts in the mouth of Eugene Wrayburn: 'I am a ridiculous fellow. Everything is ridiculous'. Dandyism can often tread a thin line between the sublime and the ridiculous. Dickens overstepped the mark.

THE SWELLS

In the 1830s and 1840s, young men at the bottom of the social scale tried to become dandies. These men, who typically worked as clerks and apprentices, lived in garrets in the backstreets of London and called themselves 'swells'. They aped the aristocratic dandies like D'Orsay, but theirs was dandyism on a budget. They hung around the cheap ready-to-wear shops, buying shoddy clothes fashioned in the foppish styles of the post-Brummell dandies like D'Orsay. Gaudily-checked trousers, colourful waistcoats, inexpensive jewellery and bright handkerchiefs marked the swells out from the crowd. The swells were ridiculed by satirists like Thackeray in *Fraser's Magazine*.

Chapter 6
FRENCH DANDIES
FROM 1800 TO 1850

It has often been claimed that Brummellian dandyism went to France in 1815 as an integral part of the Anglophilia that followed the defeat of Napoleon. To a certain extent this is true, but it must be qualified. Brummell's ascetic and quintessentially English variant of dandyism moved to France after the Napoleonic wars, but it met with a flamboyant indigenous species of the genus as soon as it crossed *la manche*. From the opulent extravagance of Louis XIV to the *égotisme* of Stendhal, the French had experienced *le dandysme* before. This native stream of extravagant French dandyism muddied the cultural waters and ensured that the dandyism borne by the tide of Anglophilia was soon unrecognisable. Indeed, it was not even recognised by Brummell when he lived in Calais.

STENDHAL

The French novelist Stendhal, born in 1783, exhibited his dandyism well before the subsequent fashion for all things English. Rooted in Romantic idealism, his dandyism was flamboyant where Brummell's was ascetic.

Stendhal, whose real name was Marie-Henri Beyle, went to Italy in 1800 with a commission to serve in the dragoons. He stayed in Milan, and his life soon revolved around music, architecture and women. He had numerous passing affairs before diving into a serious infatuation. The object of his attentions was a teenage girl named Adèle Rebuffel. In a fit of pique, Stendhal fought a duel with her fiancé and came away with the bitter taste of defeat in his mouth and a flesh wound to his foot. He decided that if he couldn't have Adèle he would settle for the next best thing – her mother. His affair with her mother continued until Stendhal caught a nasty venereal infection from a prostitute.

He resigned his commission in 1802 and lived on an allowance from his father. He hired English and Italian tutors, wrote to his sister demanding large quantities of gloves, went frequently to the theatre and took acting lessons. He tried to persuade his father to lend him money for a business venture with an old school friend, but his *père* refused to cough up the cash. Stendhal's school chum reluctantly gave him a job as a secretary.

Stendhal was soon bored by all things secretarial, so his

brother found him an administrative post in Brunswick. He was more bored there than he had been anywhere else. He returned to Paris, determined to behave with dandified affluence. He bought a *cabriolet* for the equivalent of his annual income, kept horses and servants, and owned eighteen waistcoats. Bored again, he left Paris and went on a grand tour of Bologna, Florence, Rome and Naples. When he returned he secured an appointment as a courier to Napoleon in Russia, but once again he suffered terribly from *ennui* and so returned to Paris. By 1814, his debts amounted to 37,000 francs, of which 2,000 were to his tailor.

He wrote novels in an attempt to relieve his financial troubles, but without much success. He was plagued by misfortune. The sole manuscript copy of *De l'amour* was lost in the post for eighteen months. When it was published in 1822 it sold only seventeen copies. After contemplating suicide, Stendhal resigned himself to work and got a job as a diplomat, certain that posterity would discover his genius.

HONORE DE BALZAC

Honoré de Balzac was one of the few people who noticed Stendhal's *De l'amour*, and he devoured it with glee. Balzac admired Stendhal's literary abilities and sartorial excesses, and he aped both. By December 1830, Balzac owed his tailor 904 francs — a sum well in excess of his annual budget for food and lodgings. The clothes he had bought were impressive, and the accessories spectacular. He wielded an enormous cane studded with precious stones. His new coats were embellished with elaborately carved gold buttons, and he owned a different pair of gloves for every day of the year. He equipped himself with his own coach and horses regardless of the crippling cost of this supreme act of dandyish display.

Despite his debts, which totalled 30,000 francs, Balzac had cause to be optimistic. Things were getting better. Between 1822 and 1829 he had lived in dire poverty, writing bad plays and worse novels, but in 1829 he produced his first successful book, *Les Chouans*. In 1830, Balzac was on the way up. It was time to make an impression and clothes were the way to do it, no matter how much it cost.

This ambitious young man from the provinces had always wanted to make an impression. He even changed his name from Honoré Balzac to Honoré de Balzac in order to appear more refined. From 1829 onwards he made a name for himself writing articles for chic magazines, usually about fashionable clothes and the fashionable life. One of his most memorable, 'Physiologies de la toilette,' concerned the place of the cravat in high society.

Balzac may have even been the mysterious 'H. le Blanc' who wrote a best-selling guide to cravats, detailing the ins and outs of thirty-two different knots. His full philosophy of dandyism was revealed in an article entitled 'La Traité de la vie élégante,' published in the royalist review *La Mode* in autumn 1830. He divided humanity into three categories – those who work, those who think, and those who do nothing. The dandy, he said, belonged to the third group, the only one that mattered.

From 1833 onwards, Balzac worked at a tremendous pace, fuelling his imagination with coffee made from unroasted beans, sitting at his desk throughout the night wearing his own natty variant of the dressing gown – a monk's robe. Despite this ascetic night-time attire, Balzac put forth in his writings what was immediately apparent from his day-time garb: his conviction that clothes were of great importance in the larger scheme of things. His stories are thronged with tailors, bootmakers, glovemakers and, of course, dandies. In his novel *Gobseck*, Balzac introduced us to Maxime de Trailles, 'the flower of the dandyism of that day'. 'No one wears his clothes with a finer air, nor drives a tandem with a better grace,' remarks the Comte de Born. 'It is Maxime's gift,' he continues:

> He can gamble, eat, and drink more gracefully than any man in the world. He is a judge of horses, hats, and pictures. All the women lose their heads over him. He

always spends something like a hundred thousand francs a year, and no creature can discover that he has an acre of land or a single dividend warrant. The typical knight errant of our salons, our boudoirs, our boulevards ... Maxime de Trailles is a singular being, fit for anything, and good for nothing.

In *A Distinguished Provincial at Paris*, part two of a trilogy, Balzac shows us Lucien de Rubempré at his most splendid – in Paris, shopping. We see him visit a tailor to order a waistcoat and a pair of trousers. We see him visit a linen-draper for his pocket-handkerchiefs, and a celebrated boot-maker to measure him for shoes. We see him buy a neat walking cane, gloves and shirt studs. 'In short,' says Balzac, 'he did his best to reach the climax of dandyism':

> In dress and figure he was a rival for the great dandies of the day. Lucien had wonderful canes, and a charming eyeglass; he had diamond studs, and scarf-rings and signet-rings, besides an assortment of waistcoats marvellous to behold, and in sufficient number to match every colour in a variety of costumes.

As a dandy in lifestyle as much as in costume, Lucien's time in Paris is taken up with dinner parties, champagne breakfasts, dances and balls: 'he was swept away by an irresistible current into a vortex of dissipation and easy work.'

In 1834 Balzac decided to collect together all his works of fiction as a colossal monument to his own creativity.

The sequence of novels, to be entitled *La Comédie Humaine*, would present the reader with a panoramic view of French society, and the dandy, endowed with the mock grandeur of an epic anti-hero, would be the central figure.

Honoré de Balzac

GÉRARD DE NERVAL

When the French poet, essayist, dramatist and short-story writer Gérard de Nerval was a young man, he joined the fast set. These 'Bohemians' dressed in outlandish costumes – flamboyant reds and greens, with large capes and high hats. Young Gérard, however, could always be distinguished from the rest of the group. He didn't go in for this flamboyant dandyism. His tastes were more refined. He wore a simple suit of Orléans cloth in summer and a black tailcoat in winter. His shirts and collars were invariably white.

Everything changed in 1834, when Gérard was twenty-six. He went to the Variétés theatre one night and on stage he saw an actress called Jenny. Immediately he fell in love, and he wanted Jenny to notice him. The change to his appearance was drastic. He exchanged his sober black clothes for the uniform of a Bohemian dandy. Henceforth he sported tight-fitting green trousers, a figure-hugging jacket with a high collar, patent leather shoes, and fine gloves. In this new costume he returned night after night to the Variétés theatre to watch Jenny perform.

Although he began to dress in a jolly way, Gérard's outlook on life remained rather morbid. His friends were in the habit of meeting up at a delightful cabaret, the Petit Moulin Rouge on the Avenue de la Grande Armée, for evenings of fun and light-hearted frolics. On one occasion, however, Gérard turned up with a skull that had belonged to a Drum Major killed in the battle of Moskowa.

Following Byron's example, he exhibited it to his friends, then filled it with wine and passed it round the table. This created a slightly depressing ambience, and they spent the rest of the evening talking about death.

In 1841 Gérard suffered his first attack of madness. During a Mardi Gras celebration he walked into a café and smashed all the glasses and chairs before fleeing and evading capture by hiding amidst the throng of masked revellers outside. For no apparent reason, he removed all his clothes in the middle of the street. He was arrested and taken to a police station. Spending years in and out of mental institutions took its toll on poor Gérard. Whenever he was well enough to be released, he did nothing but walk for hours on end, through night and day, throughout Paris. Living a nomadic existence, he haunted the most squalid and sordid neighbourhoods, hobnobbing with alcoholics and prostitutes. He ate less and less, and he took to sleeping on park benches. He had few clothes and fewer possessions. As he told a friend, he wore his wardrobe on his back.

Eventually he realised that he could not escape his madness. At three o'clock on a freezing cold January morning, he wandered into the Rue de la Vieille-Lanterne, a medieval alleyway inhabited mainly by ravens, and hanged himself. It seems appropriate at this stage to observe a minute of silence in remembrance of Gérard. Put the book down and count to sixty.

THEOPHILE GAUTIER

Alleged to be of Oriental ancestry, Théophile Gautier was conceived at the château d'Artagnan, the hereditary seat of the fictional hero of *The Three Musketeers*, and born on a stage prop. An intriguingly exotic man, he was considered to be the spiritual heir to d'Artagnan and he breezed through life with the flamboyance of an actor on a stage.

A childhood friend of Gérard de Nerval, who he met whilst at the Collège Charlemagne, Gautier became a member of the flashy Bohemian clique of writers which boasted Victor Hugo and Nerval himself as members. This was an auspicious start for Gautier, and it was really no surprise that he became a prominent figure for four decades in the artistic and literary life of Paris. A prolific writer, he churned out a mass of poetry, criticism, romantic novels and the occasional pornographic verse.

As a young man, he was flamboyant to excess and glorified in his reputation as a womaniser. An ardent partisan of Romanticism, he decked himself out in larger-than-life clothes. On 25th February 1830, the opening night of Hugo's *Hernani*, Gautier arrived at the theatre wearing a red waistcoat, pale green trousers with black velvet seams, a black jacket with generous velvet lapels, a grey topcoat with a green satin lining, and a black ribbon tied around his neck. His famous *gilet rouge* became a symbol of revolt, a declaration of love for the rich hedonism of art. In the late 1830s, when Théophile was at the zenith of his virile self-confidence, he revelled in his image as a flagrantly unapologetic Romantic. Ernest Feydeau, the Egyptologist, recalled Gautier's appearance: 'he grew his chestnut hair to the waist and sported a black velvet jacket with yellow Turkish babouches'.

Romanticism, Feydeau remembered, manifested itself in this period in 'the strangest kinds of eccentricity ... Everywhere people were very seriously engaged in amusing themselves.' Gautier, though eccentric, was very seriously engaged in amusing himself through the act of writing. In 1833 he published *Les Jeunes-France*, a collection of stories that celebrated and gently mocked *la vie bohème*.

Particularly worthy of note in this collection is the story 'Celle-ci et celle-là'. Rudolphe, the dandy hero of the tale, consults his mirror as his first act of the day and passes the time in leisured *ennui*. Although he is a poet, he appears never to write, and his most cheerful hours are those in which he and his friend Albert design a charming waistcoat. Rudolphe is a dandy in search of a *grande passion* – 'not a bourgeois passion, but an artist's passion, a volcanic and frenzied passion'. After failing to woo the lady of his dreams, he marries his maidservant.

In 1835 Gautier published *Mademoiselle de Maupin*, which has become his most famous novel. The preface to this novel is of crucial importance as Gautier's purest statement of *l'art pour l'art*. The novel itself is an extended manifesto of hedonistic aestheticism, beginning with dandyism as a social pose and ending with a notion of dandyism so aesthetic that it can be expressed only in works of art.

The tale is based on the adventures of the seventeenth-century bisexual Mademoiselle de Maupin who dressed and behaved like a swashbuckling swordsman and horseman, but the book begins with a portrait of the cavalier d'Albert, a snob, aesthete and fop. Wholly free from bourgeois economic pressures, d'Albert's daily chore is the graceful conquering of empty hours. He suffers from *ennui* and makes a tremendous effort with his costume and coiffure. He is vain, foppish, lethargic and nonchalant. His self-appointed task throughout the novel is to find and possess an ideal mistress – the Mademoiselle herself. In other words, d'Albert is a dandy in search of a *grande passion*. If that sounds a bit like 'Celle-ci et celle-là', then I must assure you that Gautier did have more than one plot. Besides, if you write as much as Gautier it's not surprising that certain similarities can be found between one work and another. Don't be unfair.

Théophile Gautier

BARBEY D'AUREVILLY

Born in 1808, the French novelist and critic Jules Barbey d'Aurevilly became an arbiter of social fashion and a prominent man-about-town. After studying at the Stanislas College in Paris and at the University of Caen, Barbey established himself in Paris in 1837 and tried to earn a living by writing for periodicals. Despite his poverty, he went to great lengths to establish himself as a dandy, and his sartorial splendours became legendary. He wore tight black satin trousers, blood-red gloves, long frock coats, frilly lace shirts, tall broad-brimmed hats, and bright striped capes. As Douglas Ainslie wrote in 1897, Barbey was 'for years the joy of the Parisian Boulevard. His presence in any company was a sure guarantee that the conversation would be brilliant ... With him wit went hand-in-hand with style.'

In 1845 Barbey published a volume called *Du Dandysme et de Georges Brummell*. According to Barbey's philosophy of dandyism, this complete theory of life was an artistic, intellectual and spiritual achievement. He saw the dandy as an artist with his clothes as his canvas. Dandyism, he concluded, was a moral revolt against the vulgarity and utilitarianism of a materialistic age. He saw the dandy as a timeless figure who viewed with disdain the transient ideas and tastes of his own era – 'a man who carries within himself something superior to the visible world'.

In 1868 Barbey was appointed as literary critic for *Le Constitutionnel*. He was often arbitrary, vehement, and intensely bitchy in his criticism, especially of Émile Zola and the Naturalist school, but he praised the work of his fellow dandies, notably Balzac and Baudelaire. Indeed, when Baudelaire came to propound his own theory of dandyism, his debt to Barbey was clear.

Charles Baudelaire

CHARLES BAUDELAIRE

I am led to regard external finery as one of the signs of the primitive nobility of the human soul.

CHARLES BAUDELAIRE

In *Le Peintre de la Vie Moderne*, published in 1863, Baudelaire explained his philosophy of dandyism. He saw costume as a symbol of spiritual aristocracy. The outward adornment of the dandy, he argued, was simply a sign of his inner beauty and innate superiority. 'Dandyism is not, as many shallow-minded people seem to think, merely an immoderate taste for fine dress and elegant surroundings. These things are for the true dandy only the symbols of the aristocratic superiority of his spirit.'

'To be a useful man,' he wrote in his journal, 'has always seemed to me something very vulgar.' The dandy, on the other hand, strives solely to be picturesque. He has no time for the utilitarian values of the bourgeoisie. In an untitled early poem, Baudelaire claimed that the widespread worship of Usefulness, the false god of the middle classes, was the reason that they wore such cheap and ugly clothes.

As a young man, Baudelaire's clothes were neither cheap nor ugly. 'Perfection in dress,' he wrote, 'consists in absolute simplicity, which is, indeed, the best way of being distinguished.' The contents of his wardrobe were predominantly black, although he always wore a dash of bright colour, such as a red cravat or a scarlet waistcoat. His clothes were cut according to his own instructions, a little different from the fashion of that time, with slim trousers buttoned under his shoes and an unusually long coat. His hair was long and wavy, with a full moustache and a dark, curling beard. Samuel Cramer, a dandyish character in *La Fanfarlo*, a novel of 1847, is Baudelaire's description of himself – a portrait of the artist as a young dandy.

Later in life Baudelaire decided that humanity was in decline. Progress, he thought, was a myth. Shaving off his beard and clipping his hair as short as a priest's tonsure, he abandoned the scarlet waistcoats in which he'd taken such pride and began to dress wholly in black. In the poem *Le Mauvais Moine* he chastised himself for turning into an evil monk, an ascetic who has renounced the sins of the flesh but remains obsessed with them, a reformed sinner whose sheer laziness has trapped him in a paralysis of morals.

This moral paralysis, an incapability of distinguishing good from evil, is the thread that runs through Baudelaire's major poetic work, *Les Fleurs du Mal*, which appeared in 1856. Immediately after its publication, the French government prosecuted Baudelaire on a charge of corrupting public morals. He was fined, and six of the offending poems were tactfully left out of subsequent editions. The critics and the cognoscenti, however, recognised the merits of his 'corrupt' work. Oscar Wilde praised it as 'a book that can make us live more in one single hour than life can make us live in a score of shameful years.'

In the 1850s, Baudelaire smoked opium and drank heavily, claiming that he was attracted by the aesthetic potential of these 'artificial paradises'. In 1860, inspired by Thomas De Quincey's *Confessions of an English Opium-Eater*, Baudelaire wrote *Les Paradis Artificiels*, which included a translation and commentary on De Quincey's work. During his subsequent research into the subject, he drank until he suffered brain damage and became paralysed.

Chapter 7
THE DECADENTS

The Decadents were a group of dandyish poets, novelists and artists who flourished in France during the second half of the nineteenth century and in England during the 1890s. The Decadent movement took off in France in 1856 with Baudelaire's *Fleurs du Mal* and gained momentum in the following decades with the absinthe-tinted songs of Verlaine, the inspired ravings of Rimbaud, Théophile Gautier's journal *Le Decadent* (1886-1889), and J. K. Huysmans's *A Rebours*. In England, Decadence was furthered by Ernest Dowson, Arthur Symons, Aubrey Beardsley, Oscar Wilde and *The Yellow Book*.

Decadence can be seen as the final phase of Aestheticism. The Decadents maintained the Romantics' fascination with exotic beauty, but they changed the outlook entirely. In place of the natural they prized the artificial; in place of the countryside, the city. *Ennui* is central to Decadence. The old and simple sins had lost their attractions. The Decadents always wanted to go further. Like mad Roman emperors, they demanded the perverse and the strange. Wine was not enough, so they drank absinthe. When absinthe bored them, they tried opium.

This *ennui* was born of an understanding of the futility of human existence, the realisation that man is but dust in a mindless universe. The Aesthetes thought that by being artificial we could turn meaningless lives into beautiful works of art. The Decadents realised what Oscar Wilde expressed – 'all art is quite useless'. So life is meaningless again, art is beautiful but useless, defeatism reigns, and absinthe would be delightful: yes please, I'll have a double.

Joris Karl Huysmans

JORIS KARL HUYSMANS

In Oscar Wilde's novel *The Picture of Dorian Gray*, Dorian is corrupted by a book. 'It was the strangest book that he had ever read,' wrote Wilde. 'It seemed to him that in exquisite raiment and to the sound of flutes, the sins of the world were passing in dumb show before him. Things he had dimly dreamed of were suddenly made real to him. Things of which he had never dreamed were gradually revealed.' At the time of Wilde's trial, he was asked in cross-examination to reveal the name of this hitherto nameless tome. The book, Wilde revealed, was *A Rebours* by J. K. Huysmans.

The chattering classes stopped chattering and looked nonplussed. They didn't know who Huysmans was. They imagined him to be a wealthy French hedonist and a monster of depravity. No doubt they were surprised to find out that the author of this decadent text was in fact a minor official in the French Civil Service, a junior clerk in the Ministry of the Interior. 'Joris Karl Huysmans' was a pseudonym. His real name was a little more ordinary – Charles Marie Georges Huysmans.

Huysmans's personal life, however, was anything but ordinary. A debauched misogynist of the first order, Huysmans frequented brothels and dallied with prostitutes. He held a firm belief in the purity of suffering and physical pain and a strongly held conviction in the importance of pain in religion and in art. This may have been a product of his own suffering, for throughout life he was dogged by illness. Recurrent dysentery was followed by gonorrhoea, several nervous ailments, rheumatism, and finally a permanent toothache caused by cancer of the jaw. Perhaps this is why his works are characterised by melancholy, loathing and despair.

He was contemptuous of existence and detested the insipid and mediocre spectacle of mankind. A line from one of his novels sums up his attitude: 'His contempt for humanity grew fiercer, and at last he came to realise that the world is made up mostly of fools and scoundrels.' In short, Huysmans was a grumpy old warthog. 'He speaks with an accent as of pained surprise,' reported the poet Arthur Symons, 'an amused look of contempt, so profound that it becomes almost pity for human imbecility.'

Arthur Symons remembered him well. 'I always see him in memory as I used to see him at the house of the bizarre Madame X. He leans back on the sofa, rolling a cigarette between his fingers, looking at no one, and at nothing ... with the air of one perfectly resigned to the boredom of life.' This *ennui* spilled over into the famous *A Rebours*, a work centring on the anguish of boredom.

For Arthur Symons, Huysmans's *A Rebours* was the 'unique masterpiece' of the Decadent movement, concentrating 'all that is delicately depraved, all that is beautifully, curiously poisonous in modern art'. The protagonist, Duc Jean des Esseintes, is 'a frail young man of thirty who was anaemic and highly strung, with hollow cheeks, cold eyes of steely blue, a nose which was turned up but straight, and thin, papery hands.' He is sickly, dyspeptic, a vestigial left-over of a once proud and vigorous family of wealth and influence. He suffers from horrific nightmares, numerous illnesses, headaches, and hallucinations – including, interestingly, olfactory hallucinations.

The novel is essentially a book about boredom and its appalling effects. Huysmans tells us that des Esseintes's boredom 'grew to infinite proportions':

> His soul was swept by tumultuous emotions: a longing to take vengeance for the boredom inflicted on him in the past, a craving to sully what memories he retained of his family with acts of sensual depravity, a furious desire to expend his lustful frenzy on cushions of soft flesh and to drain the sup of sensuality to its last and bitterest dregs.

Des Esseintes attempts to rid himself of this boredom with bizarre aesthetic experimentation, becoming an obsessive connoisseur of perfumes, flowers, poetry and literature, and the lengths to which he goes to relieve his boredom are extraordinary. Above all else, however, des Esseintes is a dandy and an eccentric.

He sells off his floundering estates and creates a dandy's paradise, complete with a 'symphony' of liqueur casks from which he could 'play sonatas' of drink, a tortoise encrusted with jewels, and a collection of exotic flowers chosen because they looked so outlandish and excessive they appeared to be all but artificial. 'Artifice', we are told, 'was considered by des Esseintes to be the distinctive mark of human genius.' With everything chosen with the utmost care and deliberation, des Esseintes creates a hermitage perfect in every detail. He once installed a fake church in his house in which he could receive his tradesmen:

> They used to troop in and take their places side by side in a row of church stalls; then he would ascend an imposing pulpit and preach them a sermon on dandyism, adjuring his bootmakers and tailors to conform strictly to his encyclicals on matters of cut.

His clothes are suitably exotic. As a young man he wore suits of white velvet and gold-laced waistcoats and stuck a bunch of violets in his shirtfront in lieu of a cravat. By the end of the novel, though, the reader is a little worried that this paragon of Decadence, this aesthete afflicted by *ennui*, this monster of depravity is actually…well, a bit tame and dull at heart. He keeps rearranging the books in his library. No wonder he suffers from boredom. And yes, I'll admit that Casanova too became a librarian, but that was simply his retirement job.

JEAN LORRAIN

Jean Lorrain, the French poet and novelist, chronicled the erotic, sadistic and criminal fantasies of the Decadent spirit. Born Paul Duval in 1855, his father had allowed him to pursue a literary career on condition that he use a pseudonym. Paul and his mother had leafed through a directory in search of something suitable. In 1880 he had been reborn as Jean Lorrain and had set himself up in Montmartre, eager to launch himself into the Bohemian life. He spent most of his days in a café called Le Chat Noir, an unusual place frequented by Satanists and believers in witchcraft.

In 1883 Lorrain began to frequent the salon of Charles Buet, where he met Jules Barbey d'Aurevilly, then in his seventies. Barbey still espoused his own philosophy of dandyism, and Lorrain became such a whole-hearted convert to this variety of dandyism that Remy de Gourmont later described him as 'the sole disciple of Barbey d'Aurevilly'. In 1883 Lorrain also met J. K. Huysmans at Buet's salon. Huysmans was working on *A Rebours* at the time, and it was published in the following year.

A Rebours clearly inspired Lorrain's most famous novel, *Monsieur de Phocas*, the rambling confessions of the Duc de Héneuse, who hides from society having effectively renounced his title and assumed the name 'de Phocas'. There are numerous parallels between Lorrain's Duc de Héneuse and Huysmans's Duc des Esseintes. Both characters suffer from hallucinations. Both are obsessive, cruel and nervous. Both develop a feeling of terror and suspense. Both have nervous illnesses and are haunted by sounds. Both suffer from opium dreams and disturbing visions. Both are dandies – when we first see the Duc de Héneuse he is 'neatly dressed in a myrtle-green suit and sporting a pale green silk cravat speckled with gold'.

But when compared with Lorrain's repulsive creation, Huysmans's protagonist looks especially tame and exceptionally dull. 'I am attracted and fascinated,' says the Duc de Héneuse, 'by all the acute and brutal depravity of beings reduced by wretchedness to the elementary gestures of instinct.' The decadent poet Arthur Symons said that *Monsieur de Phocas* was the most monstrous, perverse, abnormal, cruel, venomous, and infamous novel he had ever read. In other words, he loved it.

Symons was kind about the novel but unkind about the novelist: he denounced Lorrain as 'a painted dandy'. Lorrain was indeed 'painted': he rouged and powdered his face with the aim of creating a mask to prevent the world from seeing him as he really was. He consumed alcohol, cocaine and opium in alarming quantities to prevent him from seeing the world as it really was. Unsurprisingly, Lorrain was a difficult man with a bad temper. 'He was abnormally vicious, depraved and infamous,' wrote Arthur Symons. 'When I spoke with him his replies were venomous: his words stung, hurt one, they were cruel, merciless: they hit like corrosive iron.'

The singer Yvette Guilbert was not quite so harsh. 'Ah, Lorrain,' she wrote in her memoirs, 'although you were

eccentric and malicious, you could be kind and charming
and witty and distinguished – yes, distinguished even in
your misbehaviour – and I admired you and liked you, for
I could sometimes see through your mask.' Yvette Guilbert
was unusual in thinking that she could see through the
mask – especially when one remembers that Lorrain frequently failed to get on well with women. After a disastrous
affair with Judith Gautier, the daughter of Théophile
Gautier, Lorrain declared that Judith was the only woman,
save for his mother, he ever loved.

Jean Lorrain

OSCAR WILDE

Wilde was a dandy of dress, a dandy of speech, a dandy of manner, a dandy of wit, and dandy even of ideas and intellect.

MICHEÁL MACLIAMMÓIR

I have no wish to pose as being ordinary, great Heaven!

OSCAR WILDE

One of Oscar Wilde's college friends remembered him sitting awake in the early hours of the morning, talking with a burning passion about the future: 'I'll be a poet, a writer, a dramatist. Somehow or other, I'll be famous, and if not famous, notorious.' When Wilde left Oxford for London in 1878, this resolve to make himself famous was unwavering and his method of attracting attention was unflinchingly sartorial.

His clothes at Oxford had been characteristic of the time, typified by tiny bowler hats and bright tweeds cut along heavy lines. When he arrived in London, he styled himself as the Professor of Aesthetics and adopted a new costume for the part, consisting of knee breeches, silk stockings, velvet coats and flamboyant green ties of brocaded satin.

Soon Wilde was notorious. His attitudes and manners were ridiculed in *Punch* and satirised in Gilbert and Sullivan's comic opera *Patience*. His first published volume, a book of verse, came out in 1881 and sold well, despite bad reviews. He was invited to America to lecture on aesthetics, and when he returned he embarked on a series of lectures in the English provinces.

In the 1880s and the early 1890s, Wilde's doctrine of 'art for art's sake' brought back an admiration for the dandy, who does not do anything useful but is content to exist beautifully, and Wilde's works are full of such characters.

'Allow me to introduce you to Lord Goring, the idlest man in London,' announces Sir Robert Chiltern, and with this we meet the leading character of *An Ideal Husband*. Goring is the epitome of the idle dandy. His dress is the height of fashion – Wilde describes him as a 'flawless dandy' – and he spends his life flitting from fashionable salons to the fashionable clubs and back again. 'Why do you call Lord Goring good-for-nothing?' asks Mabel Chiltern. 'Because he leads such an idle life,' replies his father, Lord Caversham. 'How can you say such a thing?' asks Mabel. 'He rides in the Row at ten o'clock in the morning,' she continues, 'goes to the Opera three times a week, changes his clothes at least five times a day, and dines out every night of the season. You don't call that leading an idle life, do you?' Lord Goring has a strong hedonistic streak. When his Lord Caversham accuses him of living entirely for pleasure, the response is typically blasé: 'What else is there to live for, father?'

In *The Picture of Dorian Gray*, the eponymous anti-hero, blessed with eternal youth whilst his portrait grows old and ugly, becomes a trend-setter:

His mode of dressing, and the particular styles that from time to time he affected, had their marked influence on the young exquisites of the Mayfair balls and Pall Mall club windows, who copied him in everything that he did, and tried to reproduce the accidental charm of his graceful, though to him only half-serious, fopperies.

For Dorian, of course, this isn't enough:

In his inmost heart he desired to be something more than a mere *arbiter elegantiarum*, to be consulted on the wearing of a jewel, or the knotting of a necktie, or the conduct of a cane. He sought to elaborate some new scheme of life that would have its reasoned philosophy and its ordered principles, and find in the spiritualising of the senses its highest realisation.

This 'new scheme of life' is what Wilde calls 'the New Hedonism'. Following this creed, Dorian becomes 'more and more interested in the corruption of his own soul'. He frequents a 'sordid little room of the ill-famed tavern near the Docks' and it is rumoured that he had been seen brawling 'with foreign sailors in a low den in the distant parts of Whitechapel, and that he consorted with thieves.'

Lord Henry Wotton, the second dandy in *The Picture of Dorian Gray*, is the corrupting influence who forever changes the course of Dorian's life by giving him a copy of

Huysmans's *A Rebours*. Like Lord Goring, Henry is an idler. When we first meet him he is lying on a divan of Persian saddlebags, peering at us through thin wreaths of blue smoke from one of his opium-tainted Turkish cigarettes. 'What brings you out so early?' his father asks him. 'I thought you dandies never got up till two and were not visible till five.'

Wilde became famous, but his fame was to be his undoing. 'When the Gods wish to punish us,' said Wilde, 'they answer our prayers.' In 1895, at the peak of his career, Wilde became more than notorious. As a central figure in one of the most sensational trials of the century, he became the talk of the town, the focus of all sorts of gossip, a household word for disreputable and infamous conduct. The results of the trial scandalised the Victorian middle class. Wilde, who had been a close friend of the young Lord Alfred Douglas, was convicted of sodomy. Sentenced in 1895 to two years of hard labour in prison, he emerged physically, financially and spiritually ruined. He spent the rest of his life in Paris, using the pseudonym Sebastian Melmoth.

AUBREY BEARDSLEY

No artist of our time, none certainly whose work has been in black and white, has reached a more universal fame; none has formed for himself, out of such alien elements, a more personal originality of manner.

Arthur Symons on Beardsley

The dandy artist Aubrey Beardsley first had his work published in the spring of 1893. A year later, at the age of twenty-two, he became art editor of *The Yellow Book*. He died of consumption in March 1898 at the age of twenty-five. His productive career, then, spanned barely five years. Ever since Beardsley illustrated the English edition of *Salome*, he has been linked in the public mind with the author of that play, Oscar Wilde. But though they were friends initially, Beardsley soon began to dislike Wilde and insisted that Wilde should not be invited to contribute to *The Yellow Book*. Nevertheless, Beardsley's work has often been seen as the visual equivalent of Wilde's aesthetic manifesto, and his paradoxically beautiful yet grotesque pictures embody the striking complexities of Decadence.

Beardsley drew numerous dandified figures to display his personal commitment to dandyism. With his conspicuous features — described by Oscar Wilde as 'a face like a silver hatchet adorned by grass green hair' — and impeccable costume, Beardsley was one of the best-dressed young men in town, even if he did look a bit odd.

Scrupulously clean and meticulously attired, he usually wore discrete Baudelairean black. When he felt cheerful he wore less sombre garb: 'grey coat, grey waistcoat, grey trousers, grey suede gloves, grey felt hat, grey tie knotted wide and loose in the approved French manner.' His clothes may have been as monochrome as his illustrations, but the style was always perfect. He was, as one friend recorded, a small triumph of underplayed affectation.

Aubrey Beardsley

ARTHUR SYMONS

I have little sense of pity, but an innate sense of cruelty.
I have been cruel to many women who have clung to
me, implored my forgiveness; and I have shut my door
against them. That is, of course, because one is
wicked…Indeed, I have never known what it is to be
virtuous.

Arthur Symons on himself

In 1908, Arthur Symons suffered a severe breakdown. He
spent two years in and out of mental institutions, alternating
between moments of lucidity and attacks of paranoia.
A wreck of a man, isolated from the mainstream of the literary
world, he struggled to resume a shattered career and
was intensely fearful of recurring madness. This was a sorry
end for an influential poet, critic of the arts and theorist of
poetry who had once been a friend or acquaintance of virtually
every important French and British writer of the
time.

In happier days, Symons had been a Decadent dandy.
He espoused Decadence and wrote for *The Yellow Book* in the
1890s. He became editor of the *Savoy* in 1896. He exhibited
a Decadent and dandyish taste for the artificial and for
man's creation, the modern city. His most acclaimed essay,
'The Decadent Movement in Literature', appeared in
Harper's New Monthly Magazine in 1893. The startling manner
in which he described Decadence made him its most

important spokesman.

An exuberant womaniser, Symons balanced relationships with various dancing girls in early 1890s, occasionally infuriating one or another as a result of his casual liaisons. 'The infernal fascination of Sex,' he later wrote, 'has been my chief obsession.' His secondary obsession, it seems, was the Decadent idea of the *femme fatale*. In 1893 he met his match when he began a relationship with a ballet dancer called Lydia, a woman who obsessed him throughout his life. 'She had some evil blood in her veins,' he wrote, 'without which she could never have been so passionately, so implacably, devoted to me; bone to bone, flesh to flesh. There was something evil in both of us, which caused such terrible quarrels. She was absolutely seductive, fatally fascinating, almost shamelessly animal.'

Yvette Guilbert, a singer with whom Symons had a passionate love affair when he was in his mid-twenties, remembered his clothes many years later:

In those days he used to wear a light overcoat somewhat the colour of his hair, a poet's overcoat that had seen summers and winters, storm and shine, an overcoat that seemed to droop from much coming and going without rest. An overcoat that bore at the nape of the neck the mark of the nail from which it had hung, with pockets like open mouths waiting to be filled with beloved books, precious papers and magazines, all that intellectual food which poets have trained their pockets to accommodate. I could have picked out Arthur Symons's overcoat from a thousand others! It was symbolic, artistic ... and broke! How loveable was that overcoat, that garment of his youth! How a mere piece of clothing can stir up memories! One day Symons added to his wardrobe a gorgeous red tie, and his yellow hair and his yellow coat and that red tie made him look somewhat 'arty' and quite unforgettable.

Ernest Dowson

ERNEST DOWSON

Ernest Dowson was the Decadent poet who coined the phrase 'absinthe makes the tart grow fonder'. Dowson was a good friend of Arthur Symons – a friendship that was based on a shared predilection for unusual sensations and odd haunts. As Symons recorded, 'Sometimes, late at night, we would wander down the deserted streets near Covent Garden; where, when one drink made him unreasonable, I had to drag him bodily back from some chance encounter with the policeman.' Dowson developed a strong attachment to absinthe, but his friends always made allowances for his nascent alcoholism. 'You mustn't mind that a poet is a drunk,' said Oscar Wilde to one critic, 'rather that drunks are not always poets.' Dowson was always getting drunk and into trouble. As Symons recalled:

> Sober, Ernest was the most gentle, in manner the most gentlemanly, of men; unselfish to a fault, to the extent of weakness; a delightful companion, charm itself. Under the influence of drink, he became almost literally insane, certainly quite irresponsible. He fell into furious and unreasoning passions; a vocabulary unknown to him at other times sprang up like a whirlwind; he seemed always about to commit some act of absurd violence ... That curious love of the sordid, so common an affectation of the modern decadent, and with him so genuine, grew upon him, and dragged him into more and more sorry corners of life.

Dowson was one of those people who are only ever frowned upon by Lady Luck. Everything went wrong for the unfortunate chap. In 1894 his father died. Six months later, his mother committed suicide. He fell in love with a Polish girl whose dad owned a restaurant in Soho, but she married a waiter instead.

Dowson lived in a mouldering house in a squalid part of the East End. Never an impeccable dresser, he had ascribed to Barbey d'Aurevilly's notion of the 'dandy in creased clothes'. Eventually, however, Dowson let heedlessness develop into a total disregard of personal tidiness. Alcoholism began to destroy him. He moved to Paris, where he wandered around the city, penniless and alone, drinking absinthe by the bucket-load. In 1900, he died of tuberculosis at the age of thirty-two. Only then did Lady Luck smile.

THE YELLOW BOOK

Draw the curtains, kindle a joss stick in a dark corner, settle down on a sofa by the fire, light an Egyptian cigarette, and sip brandy and soda, as you think yourself back to the world which ended in prison and disgrace for Wilde, suicide for Crackenthorpe and John Davidson, premature death for Beardsley, Dowson and Lionel Johnson, religion for some, drink and drugs for others, temporary or permanent oblivion for many more.

Sir John Betjeman on *The Yellow Book*

The Yellow Book, the most famous of the literary magazines of the 1890s, came to be seen as epitomising its decade. Founded by John Lane, an astute entrepreneur who was acutely aware of the prevailing tastes of his day, *The Yellow Book* existed for three years and somehow summed up the spirit of Decadence.

An announcement in March 1894 gave advance warning, proclaiming that *The Yellow Book* would be 'the most interesting, unusual and important publication of its kind that has ever been undertaken. It will be charming, it will be daring, and it will be distinguished. It will be a book – a book beautiful to see … a book with style.'

When the first edition was published by Lane's Bodley Head Press in 1894, it included art by Aubrey Beardsley, an essay by Max Beerbohm entitled 'A Defence of Cosmetics', and a poem by Arthur Symons entitled 'Stella Maris', which celebrated a night spent with a prostitute. *The National Observer* said that *The Yellow Book* was 'bizarre and eccentric'. *The Westminster Gazette* called for 'an Act of Parliament to make this kind of thing illegal'. *Punch,* ready as always with an epigram and a nickname, declared that 'uncleanliness is next to Bodliness' and dubbed Aubrey Beardsley, the magazine's art editor and illustrator, 'Awfully Weirdly'.

Oscar Wilde was never invited to contribute, and this slight offended him deeply. He tried to get revenge by belittling the publication to anyone who would listen. 'It is dull and loathsome,' he told Lord Alfred Douglas, 'and it is a great failure. I am so glad.' His vitriol was of no effect and *The Yellow Book* sold in large numbers.

Unwittingly, however, Wilde became the cause of its eventual demise. On 5th April 1895, following the failure of his libel case against the Marquess of Queensbury, Wilde was arrested at the Cadogan Hotel. According to the press, he picked up a copy of *The Yellow Book* and placed it under his left arm before accompanying the police to the Bow Street police station.

John Lane was in America at the time. He asked a friend if there was any news of Wilde's libel trial. The friend passed him a newspaper with the headline 'Arrest of Oscar Wilde, Yellow Book under his arm.' Lane was horrified. 'It killed *The Yellow Book*,' he used to say, 'and it nearly killed me.' Readers of the same headline in the London papers, especially those who considered *The Yellow Book* to be depraved and immoral, reacted by besieging the offices of the Bodley Head, shouting obscenities and breaking windows.

The great irony is that the headlines were incorrect. When Wilde was arrested he was not carrying *The Yellow Book*. He was in fact carrying a French novel by Pierre Louÿs that happened to have a yellow cover. Nevertheless, there were strong protests from the Bodley Head's more conservative authors. Beardsley's designs were removed from the current edition and he was sacked as art editor. Wilde's books were also withdrawn from the company's lists. *The Yellow Book* had received a mortal blow, and soon it was dead.

Oscar Wilde

MAX BEERBOHM

Beerbohm's writing is to other men's writing as are a dandy's clothes to other men's clothes: more correct, more carefully fitted, more perfectly arranged, and regarded by him as the sign of his ineffable and invulnerable superiority to everyone else.

ROBERT VISCUSI

The young Beerbohm wore a high stiff collar, gloves, a carefully tilted silk hat, an artfully bulging frock coat and tapering trousers. He always ensured that he carried a cane. A wise decision, for accessories can make or break a man. Frank Harris noted 'a strangeness in floating tie or primrose gloves or flowered buttonhole, lending a touch of the exotic to the conventional – a sort of symbol of unique personality.' Excessively formal speech and exceptionally good manners were the finishing touches to this unique personality.

Beerbohm's first essay on dandyism, entitled 'The Incomparable Beauty of Modern Dress', appeared in 1893 in an Oxford undergraduate magazine edited by Lord Alfred Douglas. This early essay was later adapted and enlarged by Beerbohm to become 'Dandies and Dandies'. Here Beerbohm looked at the subject with impudence and detachment and snubbed self-important modernity through an ironic glorification of the Regency.

He stressed that the art of costume alone was the

essence of Brummell's dandyism. Costume was not, as Barbey d'Aurevilly had argued, an outward show of his spiritual achievement. 'Dandyism,' wrote Beerbohm, 'is ever the outcome of a carefully cultivated temperament, not part of the temperament itself.' What set Brummell apart was merely the cut of his clothes. 'The aesthetic vision of a dandy,' Beerbohm argued, 'should be bounded by his own mirror.'

Throughout the essay, Beerbohm unnerves the reader through his sly mockery of anything and everything. He laughs at Barbey, and he laughs at Brummell, but the last laugh is on Beerbohm's own contemporaries. By guileful comparisons, shifty indirection and insidious asides, he rubs the pomposity and lustre from the 'nineties. This became Beerbohm's art – the art of ridiculing, satirising, and insulting with exquisite decorum. His talents won him a place of honour in the first *Yellow Book*, when he was still an undergraduate and only twenty-one.

Beerbohm was a great enough mind to see both the wonder and the absurdity of the dandy. In his celebrated tale 'Enoch Soames' (1912), he recounts the story of the eponymous would-be decadent and his inability to make the grade as either dandy or artist. Soames is an execrable affected poet of *The Yellow Book* period. Despite hailing from Preston, he feels qualified to call Baudelaire 'a bourgeois in spite of himself' and has the audacity to say it in French too.

Out of vanity, Soames makes a pact with the devil and in return for his soul he is allowed to go a hundred years into the future to see how posterity has viewed his talent. Once he has travelled forwards in time, Soames goes to the British Library to check his name on the catalogue. The only record of him is as a fictional character in a story by Max Beerbohm.

Beerbohm writes the tales as a *faux-memoir*, placing himself within the drama. He first encounters Soames whilst drinking vermouth with William Rothenstein at that Mecca of fin-de-siècle dandies, the Café Royal, describing him thus:

> Rather tall, very pale, with longish and brownish hair, he had a thin vague beard – or rather, he had a chin on which a large number of hairs weakly curled and clustered to cover its retreat. He was an odd-looking person; but in the 'nineties odd apparitions were more frequent, I think, than they are now. The young writers of that era – and I was sure this man was a writer – strove earnestly to be distinct in aspect. This man had striven unsuccessfully. He wore a soft black hat of the clerical kind but of Bohemian intention, and a grey waterproof cape which, perhaps because it was waterproof, failed to be romantic.

The only really successful dandy of the story is the devil himself. Here Beerbohm recounts his final encounter with the sulphurous rake:

> I was walking, one afternoon, along the Rue d'Antin, when I saw him advancing from the opposite direction

— over-dressed as ever, and swinging an ebony cane, and altogether behaving as though the whole pavement belonged to him. At the thought of Enoch Soames and the myriads of other sufferers eternally in this brute's dominion, a great cold wrath filled me, and I drew myself up to my full height. But — well, one is so used to nodding and smiling in the street to anybody whom one knows, that the action becomes almost independent of oneself: to prevent it requires a very sharp effort and great presence of mind. I was miserably aware, as I passed the Devil, that I nodded and smiled to him. And my shame was the deeper and hotter because he, if you please, stared straight at me with the utmost haughtiness. To be cut — deliberately cut! — by him. I was, I still am, furious at having had that happen to me.

The absurd hero of *Zuleika Dobson*, Beerbohm's great dandy novel, is almost as ridiculous as Enoch Soames. John Albert Edward Claude Orde Angus Tankerton Tanville-Tankerton, the fourteenth duke of Dorset, is astoundingly wealthy, phenomenally gifted, consummately dandified — and utterly insufferable. 'It was as a Knight of the Garter that he had set the perfect seal on his dandyism,' Beerbohm tells us:

Yes, he reflected, it was on the day when first he donned the most grandiose of all costumes, and wore it grandlier than ever yet in history had it been worn, than ever would it be worn hereafter, flaunting the robes with a grace unparalleled and inimitable, and lending, as it were, to the very insignia a glory beyond their own, that he once and for all fulfilled himself, doer of that which he had been sent into the world to do.

'A dandy he had lived,' says Beerbohm, 'and in the full pomp and radiance of his dandyism he would die.'

According to Logan Persall Smith, Beerbohm always loved to be idle: 'As to the loafing, there could be no question; I have never known a more wisely idle person ... He was quite content, so far as I could see, to live on the most modest of incomes and do nothing all day long.' Content to do nothing, Beerbohm's dandyism 'reduced at last, in his life and writings, to the simple fact of a well-ordered existence made up of little things which gentlemen take for granted,' argued the scholar of dandyism Ellen Moers. 'Politeness, personal dignity, care in the choice of spoken and written word, formality of dress: the artificial props of the civilised world were the handful of Beerbohm's principles.'

Beerbohm felt that he 'could have no part in Modern Life'. He looked back to the Golden Days of dandyism – not to the flamboyant dandyism of Romanticism, not to the intellectual dandyism of Baudelaire, not to the corrupt dandyism of Decadence, but to the oldest form of the tradition, the dandyism of pose and poise, the dandyism of the gentleman. The gentleman, he sadly intoned, was

a now extinct species, a lost relic of the eighteenth century and of the days before the great Reform Bill of

1832; a leisurely personage, attired with great elaboration, on his way to one of his many clubs; not necessarily interesting in himself; but fraught with external character and point: very satisfactory to those for whom the visible world exists. From a sociological standpoint perhaps he was all wrong, and perhaps his successor – the earnest fellow ... hurrying along to his job – or in quest of some job – is all right. But one does rather wish the successor looked as if he felt himself to be all right.

Max Beerbohm

Chapter 8
THE EDWARDIAN DANDIES AND BEYOND

Those years before the war were, of all the years since the days of the Regency Bucks, the halcyon time for rich young bachelors. In the early part of the reign of Queen Victoria – that unutterable woman – the world stood upon lavender-scented stilts ... But the Accession of King Edward changed all that, and young men came into their own if they possessed an adequate income. My income being on an admirable scale I quickly settled down to the life of the *jeunesse dorée* ... I had chambers in Albany, an account at half a dozen Bond Street jewellers, a rapidly improving taste in orchids, a handsome Napier motorcar, and the acquaintance of half the stage-doorkeepers in the West End ... our money, our youthful good looks and high spirits, our titles and our titled friends, our unlimited leisure, all combined to make the second and third rows of the chorus easy game for us.

A. G. MACDONELL, *The Autobiography of a Cad*

EDWARD VII

When the gloom of the Victorian age lifted, Britain stepped into a bright new era. The Decadence of the fin-de-siècle dandies looked dated. Dandyism reinvented itself once again in the image of the king who led very much from the front.

Edward VII, who reigned until 1910, brought a dandified roguishness back to the Royals and inaugurated a period of carefree hedonism. Bertie, as Edward was known, had always enjoyed dressing well and pursuing pleasure. He lived a life of immaculate tailoring (courtesy of Savile Row), smoking, drinking, gambling, gluttony and womanising. After getting a taste for the bachelor high life at Oxford, he continued unabated in London and on the Continent. He loved the demi-monde of Paris and the French Riviera. Despite marrying in 1863, he carried on affairs with married women and liaisons with prostitutes and actresses. Henry James dubbed him 'the arch vulgarian, Edward the Caresser'.

He had an extreme and passionate influence in uniforms and once claimed that an entire evening had been spoilt by the fact that one of his guests had worn the wrong tie. His lasting mark on matters sartorial was his habit of leaving the last button on his waistcoats undone – largely, it is thought, because he was too portly in his later years to fasten it. No matter – people at the time saw it as a deliberate affectation of style and followed suit.

MILITARY DANDIES

The First World War placed the military dandy at the centre of the international stage. General Alexander, for example, was something of an aesthete who wore a fur muff even in the trenches. The hell of war did not distract the members of the officer class from the matter of appearance, despite the fact that most of the infantry was simply too muddy to care. The most dandified regiment was the Grenadier Guards, who wore very expensive, colourful, close-fitting uniforms. The life of the Guards officers after the War became one of alternate ritual and idleness. There was four months annual leave for captains, five for majors and six for colonels. Their work was to guard the palaces, the Tower of London, and so on. They observed certain aristocratic customs and codes of behaviour peculiar to themselves. A Guard officer, for example, would never carry a case or a parcel, smoke a Virginian cigarette, or reverse in waltzing. This was the heyday of the military dandy.

THE BRIGHT YOUNG THINGS

By the 1920s the huge psychological scars left by the war were gradually receding and the next generation of youth was soon ready to have fun again. And so this era saw the emergence of the so-called Bright Young Things. According to Cecil Beaton, it became fashionable to say 'madly' and 'divine' and 'how terribly unfunny, darling'. The dandies clipped their speech as they turned their toes in. People imitated Philip Sassoon, who emphasised each syllable equally, saying 'I could-dern't care less' and 'I could-dern't agree more'.

Brian Howard was the typical Bright Young Thing. He went to Eton and Oxford with Harold Acton, and followed Acton to London in 1925. Howard was supposed to be studying law, but he spent most of his time studying ballet. In 1930 he was commissioned to edit an anthology of post-war poets, but it was never done. Instead he wrote his own poetry, and his first and only volume, *God Save the King*, came out in 1931. Howard lived up to the Wildean ideal of a young man 'with a perfect profile and no profession'. After his suicide in 1958, his obituary in *The Times* concluded thus:

In the small world of Eton and Oxford during the 1920s, it seemed inevitable that Brian Howard would emerge as one of the eminent figures of his generation.

Exotically handsome, after the manner of a Disraeli hero, rich, brilliant in conversation, and endowed with great physical courage, he only needed the right spur to set him on the ladder of fame.

The Bright Young Things ensured that the cocktail party, which Alec Waugh is credited with inventing in 1924, became tremendously popular. At the Sailor Party, given by Brian Howard at the swimming baths in Buckingham Palace Road, flowers were strewn in the water. A Circus Party was held in 1928, and a Boat Party and a Cowboy Party in 1929. The most spectacular was the Great Urban Dionysia, given by Babe Plunket-Greene for Brian Howard on his twenty-fourth birthday in 1929. The White Party, given by Sandy Baird, one of Brian's friends, ended disastrously with the death of a young man in suspicious circumstances. Such things were to be expected. These parties were as well known for their sordid aftermaths as they were for their ornate invitations.

The period between the turn of the century and the outbreak of the Second World War was a Golden Age of British dandyism. The 1920s, in particular, was an astounding decade. Noel Coward rose to fame, Fred Astaire danced on the stage in London, and William Gerhardie and Ronald Firbank published their best works. This was an era when dandies were kings and kings were dandies.

HAROLD ACTON

Dandy and aesthete Harold Acton was known for his cultured and eccentric nature. Acton was educated at Eton and at Christ Church, Oxford, where he lived in the neo-Gothic Meadow Building in a room filled with Victorian bric-a-brac with a balcony overlooking the meadows, giving him a splendid view towards the river. He bought a grey bowler, jackets with broad lapels and countless pairs of broad pleated trousers. Each new pair of trousers was broader than the last, eventually becoming so wide that they flapped around and created an illusion of swaying. People felt seasick whenever Acton sauntered past. Nevertheless, the trend had been set and soon these trousers – nicknamed 'Oxford bags' – were worn by all the young blades in town.

Tom Driberg, who came up to Christ Church two years later than Acton, and who eventually became a gossip columnist for The *Daily Express*, remembered going to Hall Brothers, the Oxford tailors on the High, to order 'trousers very wide and flapping at the ankles, far wider than the navy's bell bottoms … and in an unusual colour – bright green.' Incidentally, Driberg's trousers met with an unfortunate end – a gang of drunken 'hearties' raided his room one night, 'de-bagged' him and tore the offending item of clothing to shreds.

Whilst at Oxford, Acton attracted a circle of undergraduates, not least for reciting 'The Waste Land' through a megaphone at a garden party in Worcester College. Two old ladies were alarmed by this method of recital, but they thought that this young man had a 'nice, kind face' and they didn't want to hurt his feelings by getting up and leaving openly. They were obliged, therefore, to sink to their knees and creep away on all fours.

The megaphone soon became Acton's symbol. When his first volume of poems, *Aquarium*, was published in his second term, he took the megaphone with him wherever he went. 'Since I was free from false modesty,' he said, 'and possessed a resonant voice, I never faltered when asked to read them, but shouted them lustily down a megaphone. Nor would I tolerate interruptions.' The megaphone, he added, 'could also be brandished as a weapon.' On a number of occasions, he stood on his balcony and read poetry through his megaphone to groups of people in the meadow below.

Acton served as the model for the Evelyn Waugh's dandies Anthony Blanche in *Brideshead Revisited* and Ambrose Silk in *Put Out More Flags*. In fact, Waugh's descriptions of Blanche and Silk stand as perfect portraits of the young Acton, down to the eccentricities. Anthony Blanche recites *The Waste Land* through a megaphone in Sebastian's room in Christ Church's Meadow Building, moving onto the balcony to regale 'the sweatered and muffled throng that was on its way to the river'. Similarly, Ambrose Silk recites *In Memoriam* through a megaphone whilst a student at Oxford.

AMBROSE SILK

Two soldiers outside a public house made rude noises
as Ambrose passed. 'I'll tell your sergeant-major of
you,' he said gaily, almost gallantly, and flounced down
the street. I should like to be one of them, he thought.
I should like to go with them and drink beer and make
rude noises at passing aesthetes.

EVELYN WAUGH, *Put Out More Flags*

Ambrose Silk, a central character in Evelyn Waugh's *Put Out
More Flags*, is the archetypal dandy in the early twentieth-
century mould – the effeminate aesthete, the embodiment
of dandyism after the fall of Oscar Wilde. This dandyism
had become 'the current exchange of comedians,' but
Waugh intends that we should ignore this plebeian sniggering and see something glorious, timeless and noble in
Ambrose's individuality. Ambrose's friends look on him as
a 'survival from *The Yellow Book*' with 'the swagger and flash
of a young Disraeli'.

He wears 'a dark, smooth suit that fitted perhaps a little closely at the waist and wrists, a shirt of plain, cream
coloured silk; and a dark, white spotted bow tie'. It is when
Ambrose describes himself, however, that he embodies
Waugh's notion of the dandy – an ideal owing more to
attributes than to apparel. His dandyism manifests itself as
'a habit of dress, a tone of voice, an elegant, humorous
deportment that had been admired and imitated, a swift,

epicene felicity of wit, the art of dazzling and confusing those he despised'. In Waugh's mind the dandy must have intelligence, wit and a certain reckless eccentricity.

After being given a position as the sole representative of Atheism in the religious department of the Ministry of Information, Ambrose – an author by profession – decides to start a magazine to keep culture alive. For this magazine, he writes a fifty-page story entitled 'A Monument to a Spartan'. This 'major work of Art' is the autobiographical tale of Ambrose's unsuccessful romance with a German named Hans which fell apart when Hans became a Nazi and could no longer associate with the Jewish Ambrose Silk.

Misfortune arrives in the guise of Ambrose's erstwhile friend, the caddish Basil Seal. Basil, who works at the War Office, has been told that he will be promoted to a Captain of the Marines if he catches a fascist. Basil decides that it would be easier to catch someone he already knows, so he tricks Ambrose into rewriting the ending of 'A Monument to a Spartan'. 'Why don't you leave it like that, with Hans still full of his illusions, marching into Poland in the first exhilaration of victory?' Basil asks.

Ambrose changes the ending accordingly, so that 'to anyone ignorant of Ambrose's private history it bore one plain characteristic – the triumphant paean of Hitler Youth.' Almost too late, Basil realises the outcome of his prank, and – as the men of Scotland Yard close in – helps Ambrose escape to Ireland dressed as a priest. 'But Basil,' objects Ambrose on being told that he cannot take his Charvet ties and his crêpe-de-Chine pyjamas, 'I must have

169

some clothes'. And so Ambrose Silk, following the example of Brummell before him, goes into exile.

For Ambrose, the fact that he suffers for his Art is a complete vindication of his artistic ideals: 'it was something inalienable from his state; the artist's birthright'. He is, even in exile, the perfect representative of a spirited and resplendent dandyism:

> Sitting there, gesticulating very slightly, raising his voice occasionally in a suddenly stressed uncommon epithet or in a fragment of slang absurdly embedded in his precise and literary diction, giggling between words now and then as something which he had intended to say changed shape and became unexpectedly comic in the telling – Ambrose like this caused time to slip back to an earlier age ... when amid a more splendid décor of red plush and gilt caryatides fin-de-siècle young worshippers crowded to the tables of Oscar and Aubrey.

ANTHONY BLANCHE

Anthony Blanche, aesthete and dandy par excellence, floats through the first part of Evelyn Waugh's *Brideshead Revisited* with a leer, a wink and a knowing giggle. He arrives at Sebastian Flyte's luncheon party and immediately takes charge — 'talking in a luxurious, self-taught stammer; teasing; caricaturing the guests at his previous luncheon; telling lubricious anecdotes of Paris and Berlin; and doing more than entertain; transfiguring the party, shedding a vivid, false light of eccentricity upon everyone.' He moved, our narrator tells us, 'with his own peculiar stateliness, as though he had not fully accustomed himself to coat and trousers and was more at ease in heavy, embroidered robes.'

Blanche grew up as a 'nomad of no nationality'. After two years at Eton, he travelled the world with his mother and her Pekinese, spending time in hotels, furnished villas, spas, casinos and beaches. He had dined with Proust and Gide, but 'was on closer terms with Cocteau and Diaghilev'. He had, we are told, 'been cured of drug-taking in California and of an Oedipus complex in Vienna'.

Having grown up quickly in exotic surroundings, Blanche has become 'as ageless as a lizard, as foreign as a Martian' — and as omniscient as the outlandish god of some corrupt civilisation. He delights in making it known that the wisdom of the world is in his possession: 'you only had to mention the name of your bootmaker for him to recommend an Armenian at Biarritz who catered especially for fetishists, or to name a house where you had stayed, for him to describe a place he frequented in Madrid.'

It is no surprise that his peers felt like children beside him: 'while we had been rolling one another in the mud at football and gorging ourselves with crumpets, Anthony had helped oil fading beauties on sub-tropical sands and had sipped his aperitif in smart little bars'. Our narrator tells us that Anthony's vices flourished 'less in the pursuit of pleasure than in the wish to shock', but we are by no means shocked when Anthony runs off to Germany to live with a policeman. The only shocking thing about it is that this exotic creature has lapsed into happy domesticity.

SEBASTIAN FLYTE

The dandyish Sebastian Flyte in Evelyn Waugh's *Brideshead Revisited* appears in 'dove-grey flannel, white crêpe-de-chine, and a Charvet tie'. He invariably carries his teddy bear, Aloysius, of whom he is very fond. 'I have a good mind not to take Aloysius to Venice', he tells our narrator Charles Ryder. 'I don't want him to meet a lot of horrid Italian bears and pick up bad habits.' Charles first meets Sebastian when the latter is sick through the former's window, and they soon become friends.

On a glorious summer day, Sebastian and Charles sit under a clump of elms where they eat strawberries and drink wine. They light fat Turkish cigarettes and lie on their backs, 'while the blue-grey smoke rose, untroubled by any wind, to the blue-green shadows of the foliage, and the sweet scent of the tobacco merged with the sweet summer scents around us and the fumes of the sweet, golden wine seemed to lift us just a finger's breadth above the turf and hold us suspended.'

Sebastian increasingly turns to drink. 'I began to realise,' says our narrator, 'that Sebastian was a drunkard in quite a different sense to myself. I got drunk often, but through an excess of high spirits, in the love of the moment, and the wish to prolong and enhance it; Sebastian drank to escape.'

WILLIAM GERHARDIE

William Gerhardie was born in St Petersburg in 1895, the youngest son of a British industrialist. Educated in Russia with English as his fourth (and weakest) language, his family didn't rate his prospects too highly and he was sent to London in his late teens to prepare for a commercial career. Yet he dreamt only of marrying a rich bride whose wealth would allow him the leisure he desired to become a literary dandy in the mould of Oscar Wilde. He served in the Royal Scots Greys during the First World War, arriving at his barracks brandishing an elegant cane and long hair under a modish bowler hat. He was posted to the staff of the British Military attaché in St Petersburg, and then to the British Military Mission in Serbia, before returning to England.

Whilst studying Russian at Worcester College, Oxford, he published his first novel, *Futility*. He soon became one of the most lavishly praised and influential novelists of the 1920s. 'I have talent,' commented Evelyn Waugh, 'but he has genius.' The peak of his success came in 1925 with the publication of his masterpiece, *The Polyglots*. Most of the heroes in his novels are thinly veiled versions of himself who spout epigrammatic wit and offer an engagingly absurd view of the world.

In *The Polyglots*, the hero Captain George Hamlet Alexander Diabologh, a dryly conceited young chap staying abroad in an absurd world, is in love with himself and is

174

reprimanded throughout the novel for regarding himself unduly in any mirror he passes · — though he is by all accounts an ordinary looking chap. 'Women like me,' he says. 'My blue eyes, which I roll in a winning way when I talk to them, look well beneath my dark brows — which I daily pencil. My nose is remotely tilted, a little arched. But what disposes them to me, I think, are my delicate nostrils, which give me a naïve, tender, guileless expression, like this — 'M'm' — which appeals to them.'

Diabologh is a desk-bound soldier, yet exceptionally proud of the three pips on his shoulder, his spurs and his cavalry boots. He also has in his kit an ancient and useless ceremonial sword bought cheap in the Charing Cross Road. It makes him look ridiculous as it is far too long even when he is sat on his horse.

Despite his egotism, however, Diabologh has the dandy's witheringly cynical view of the world, especially when answering enquiries about his rank: 'I owe my recent promotion,' he says, 'to having, at a psychological moment, slapped a certain War Office Colonel on the shoulder: just as his ego touched the height of elation. Had I slapped him a second too early or a second too late, my military career would have taken a different course altogether. I am sure of it.'

William Gerhardie travelled widely in Europe, America and India, became a protégé of Lord Beaverbrook, an epic seducer of women, a renowned literary wit, and a celebrity on the glitterati cocktail circuit. He remained prolific throughout the 1920s and 1930s and precociously published his memoirs at the age of thirty-five. He published nothing after 1940 and increasingly lived like a hermit in his bachelor pad in London's West End, sinking into obscurity. During the Blitz, he sat in his flat with a large saucepan on his head. He dressed strangely and pursued dietary and spiritualist fads. He invented a lotion for baldness, a self-pasting toothbrush, and a cocktail called 'Sherrivapa' made from sherry and evaporated milk. To the end he remained something of an alien.

RONALD FIRBANK

'O, help me heaven,' she prayed, 'to be decorative and to do right.'

RONALD FIRBANK

Ronald Firbank, an English writer of the early twentieth century, was a dandy of a fragile and eccentric nature. His mother was the society beauty Harriet Jane Garrett. His father was the MP Sir Thomas Firbank, a wealthy company director, and his grandfather was Joseph Firbank, who had built up the family's fortune as a railway contractor.

Sunstroke as a child left Ronald rather delicate, and from an early age he liked to spend much of his time alone. As a young man he went to Trinity Hall, Cambridge, where his select coterie included Rupert Brooke and Oscar Wilde's son Vyvyan Holland.

Ronald left Cambridge in 1909 without completing a degree and travelled around Spain, Italy, the Middle East, and North Africa. Returning to London, he lived the life of a leisured aesthete and became a *habitué* of the Café Royal, the literary haunt in Regent Street.

Firbank's aestheticism was at times vehement. He despised people whose feeling for beauty was not as strong as his own, and when drunk he refused to speak to ugly people. Ifan Kyrle Fletcher said that Ronald was nervously self-conscious but that he concealed this trait 'behind a barrier of reserve, when his gestures grew long and sinuous and his voice slithered without control over his sentences'. He had an impish sense of the ridiculous, and revelled in grotesque ornamentation.

His clothes, although made by the best tailors, always looked a little foreign. He dressed in a dark well-fitting lounge suit, and he wore a black bowler. He carried gloves and a cane. His hands were white and very well kept and bejewelled with ornate rings. He stained his fingernails crimson. 'Before my wife and I learned his name,' recorded C. W. Beaumont, a bookseller in Charing Cross Road, 'we always spoke of him as "the man with red nails".'

The fact that his family was extremely wealthy relieved Ronald from the need to get a job and enabled him to pay for the publication of his own works. This was necessary as his unconventional lifestyle and his open homosexuality caused him to be denounced by the critics and ignored by the reading public of his day. Consequently most of his work appeared only in expensive limited editions.

A master of irreverent wit and social parody, he cultivated a beautiful and highly individual prose style. Influenced by Wilde and Beardsley, he saw the glint and shimmer in the rotten fruit of Decadence and with his discerning eye it was transformed into a hoard of exquisite jewels.

With no conventional plots, his novels are disciplined journeys into elegant and fantastic worlds inhabited by bizarre characters – society ladies, ecclesiastics, lesbians, kings and nuns – and full of sexual innuendo, covert meanings and black humour. Vyvyan Holland described his books as 'the product of dreams, written in that nebulous state of mind one is in just before fully regaining consciousness, while the dream still holds one with its spell, and its improbability and absurdity are not yet apparent.'

Amongst the most famous are *Vainglory*, published in 1915, and *Valmouth*, published in 1919. His novel *Sorrow in Sunlight*, printed in 1924, appeared in the USA under the title *Prancing Nigger*. The masterful tale *Concerning the Eccentricities of Cardinal Pirelli*, published in 1926, concerns the demise of a priest while chasing an appealing choirboy around the altar.

Firbank developed a number of eccentricities. He kept a solitary plant in his flat and employed a gardener to come in twice a day to water it. He wrote all his novels on piles of deep blue cards. In London he claimed to eat nothing but strawberries washed down with champagne, and when he moved to Rome it was rumoured that he ate nothing but rose petals. His strange eating habits had a rather consumptive effect and he died in Rome in 1926.

SAKI

Otherwise known as Hector Hugh Munro, Saki is the genius of Edwardian literary brevity who wrote delightful short stories featuring idle young dandies like Clovis and Reginald. Their world is one of unrelenting leisure, and they flit from sleepy London clubs to weekend parties in the country, taking tea with articulate duchesses and chattering in drawing rooms. These effete and lazy aesthetes glide through these realms of upper-crust tranquillity, so bored that all they can do to alleviate their *ennui* is speak in epigrams and cause chaos by means of elaborate hoaxes and practical jokes. Their pranks upset maiden aunts and rub dusty old majors up the wrong way.

Reginald, like Clovis, is known for his waistcoats and 'has a magnificent scorn for details, other than sartorial'. All they care about is their own meticulous grooming, impeccable tastes and continually deferred literary ambitions. 'One of these days,' says Reginald, 'I shall write a really great drama. No one will understand the drift of it, but everyone will go back to their homes with a vague feeling of dissatisfaction with their lives. Then they will put up new wallpaper and forget.' Both Reginald and Clovis are convinced that they have extraordinary talents in the writing of poetry. Reginald's 'Hymn to the New Year' is, if nothing else, astounding:

Have you heard the groan of a gravelled grouse,
Or the snarl of a snaffled snail?
Have you lain a-creep in the darkened house
Where the wounded wombats wail?

'I felt worked up now and then at the thought of that house with the stricken wombats in it,' says Reginald. 'It simply wasn't nice.' But nothing can beat Clovis's 'Durbar Recessional' for sheer poetic extravagance:

The amber dawn-drenched East with sun-shafts kissed,
Stained sanguine apricot and amethyst,
O'er the washed emerald of the mango groves
Hangs a mist of opalescent mauves,
While painted parrot-flights impinge the haze
With scarlet, chalcedon and chrysoprase.

Reginald's 'Peace Poem' begins with a 'widgeon westward winging'. 'Why widgeon?' asks his friend. 'Why not?' replies Reginald. 'Anything that winged westward would naturally begin with a w.' 'Need it wing westward?' persists his friend. 'The bird must go somewhere. You wouldn't have it hang around and look foolish,' Reginald answers. After further discussion, Reginald asks his friend if he would like to hear another stanza of the Peace Poem. 'If I must make a choice,' the friend replies, 'I think I would rather they went on with the war.'

CEDRIC HAMPTON

The character of Basil Seal in Evelyn Waugh's *Put Out More Flags* was based on Peter Rodd, a rogue who Waugh had known at Oxford. Rodd married Nancy Mitford, a novelist who was very much attached to the Bright Young Things. In her novel *Love in a Cold Climate* she created Cedric Hampton, perhaps the brightest of all the young things. The dazzling Cedric is an extravagant fop whose rise is quite unexpected. As Lord Montdore's only male heir, Cedric Hampton inherits the family fortune. Lord Montdore's family is horrified. They have never met Cedric. Indeed, they don't know anything about him, beyond a vague notion that he grew up in Nova Scotia. They expect him to be an uncultured backwoodsman, but they couldn't be more wrong.

Cedric is a dandy par excellence. He sails into the room as 'a glitter of blue and gold' and immediately makes himself at home. It emerges that he has lived in Europe, having moved to Paris aged eighteen. 'I was sent to Paris to learn some horrid sort of job,' he reveals, 'I quite forget what, as I never had to go near it. It is not necessary to have jobs in Paris, one's friends are so very very kind.' He is an arbiter of taste, an energetic arranger of festivities and a connoisseur of fine *objets d'art*. 'I need a very great deal of beauty round me,' he says, 'beautiful objects wherever I look and beautiful people who see the point of One.'

He is described as 'a human dragonfly'. We see him in

a pale mauve silk dressing gown, and he is very fond of suits with seams piped in contrasting shades. He wears a green linen coat with brown piping on the seams, and on another occasion he sports a coarse blue tweed suit piped with scarlet. Some members of the Montdore family get on well with the new arrival, but not everyone is keen:

> There was a terrible scene at the Oxford platform one day. Cedric went to the bookstall to buy *Vogue*, having mislaid his own copy. Uncle Matthew, who was waiting there for a train, happened to notice that the seams of his coat were piped in a contrasting shade. This was too much for his self-control. He fell upon Cedric and began to shake him like a rat; just then, very fortunately, the train came in, whereupon my uncle, who suffered terribly from train fever, dropped Cedric and rushed to catch it. 'You'd never think,' as Cedric said afterwards, 'that buying *Vogue Magazine* could be so dangerous. It was well worth it though, lovely Spring modes.'

EDWARD VIII

Edward VIII, formerly the Prince of Wales, and later, after his abdication, the Duke of Windsor, was a notorious clotheshorse and a right royal dandy. 'There was something so nice about his clothes,' remembered Reverend Philip Clayton, who ran a hostel for troops during World War I. 'I don't know where he lived, but he was always so nice and clean.'

It was at Oxford that the Prince's fascination with clothing first developed. The seed of his life's interest was planted under the dreaming spires, and henceforth he took great pleasure in his own clothes and studied the history and evolution of costume. In his book, *A Family Album*, which he intended to be a book of memoirs, he returns compulsively to the subject of clothes time after time, until the book almost turns into a history of modern dress.

When the Prince went to university, he sported all the latest fashions – flannel trousers with sports coats, plus-fours, and trousers with turn-ups. He demonstrated a fondness for checks, plaids, bright colours and loud tweeds. The Prince adopted a raffish air and persisted in wearing his top hat on the side of his head when out hunting – 'a thing,' says the historian Frances Donaldson, 'that even schoolboys at Eton or Harrow knew was done only by cads.' He wore brown and white brogues – 'a totally reliable sign of a cad,' says Donaldson.

His interest in clothing never abated, and he persisted in wearing bright colours. Years after his abdication, Diana

Hood remembered seeing him in his garden in France wearing crimson trousers with a light blue shirt and red and white shoes one day, and bright blue trousers with a canary yellow shirt and blue shoes the next. His vivid azure socks once shocked Lady Diana Cooper. More importantly, however, the Prince was an innovator, and he invented a new way of tying a necktie, the Windsor knot.

The Prince's influence was as important as his innovation. He set fashions, and everyone who wanted to cut a dash imitated his style. During Fred Astaire's first trip to England in 1923, for example, the Prince of Wales changed Fred's way of dressing entirely. It would be no exaggeration to say that the Prince created the Astaire trademark of top hat and tails.

In 1923, the Prince saw Fred and his sister Adele on stage in *Stop Flirting* and was hooked. He thought that this brother-and-sister dancing team from the States was the best thing since loudly-checked tweed suits. The Prince returned to see the show a second time, and invited Fred and Adele to the Riviera Club for cocktails afterwards. That evening, the Prince was wearing white tie and tails with an intriguing small white waistcoat featuring tiny lapels. Fred was fascinated.

Next morning, when Adele was sleeping off her hangover, Fred went to Hawes and Curtis, the tailors who made the Prince's waistcoats. 'I'd like a waistcoat like that of the Prince of Wales,' said Fred. 'I'm sorry, sir,' replied the tailor, 'but we can't possibly discuss any clothes that we have made for other customers.'

Undeterred, Fred walked a few doors down, to Anderson and Shepherd, who also made clothes for the Prince. Fred had learnt his lesson, and this time he knew what to do. 'I'd like a small white waistcoat with tiny lapels,' he said. 'Look, I'll draw what it should look like.' The tailor was happy to oblige. The rest, as they say, is history.

But Edward was something more than an ultra-fashionable English gentleman in loud tweeds. Due to his irrepressible independence, he reigned for less than a year. A gentleman would not have abdicated the throne of England to marry Wallis Simpson, a twice-divorced American, but a dandy would – and, as a dandy, he did.

CECIL BEATON

Cecil Beaton cast himself as a dandy not just in the superficial sense of one who paid undue attention to his clothes and grooming, but in the more complex sense of one who desired a role for himself as the eternal outsider, the ironic, detached observer.

Philippe Garner

When the English photographer and theatrical designer Cecil Beaton was a young man, he reinvented himself as a dandy. A man of considerable and distinctive elegance, he soon became known for the studied stylishness of his dress. In later years he adopted wide-brimmed hats, foppish cravats and tailored jackets.

In the 1930s he worked as a photographer for *Vogue* and in 1954 he published *The Glass of Fashion*, a lively account of women's fashions in the first half of the twentieth century. It is as a photographer of celebrities, however, that he is remembered. His life's work recorded the extravagances, vanities and artificiality of the worlds of aristocratic privilege, artistic salons, fashion, film and theatre.

Beaton's photographs are reflections of a highly refined sensibility, reflections of a dandy's aesthetic yearning for perfect beauty. This concern for style, for appearances and for pose was evident from the outset. It was manifest in the dandyish photographs from the early 1920s of Rex Whistler wearing knee breeches and holding a guitar, reclining under a tree. It was apparent in photographs from the 1930s in which Jean Cocteau adopts a raffish pose, holding suede gloves and a cane. A dandy's creative output is only ever a reflection of his greatest works of art – himself and his life – and this has never been more true than in the case of Cecil Beaton.

Cecil Beaton's writings – especially his diaries – are extremely entertaining, and his opinions with regard to his friends and lovers were often very brutal. After Cecil was seduced by Fred Astaire's sister, Adele, he was less than complimentary about her. 'She is rather too roguish but a delightfully brittle puppet,' he wrote in *Vogue*. 'I admire her ugly face,' he wrote in his diary. The novelist William Gerhardie described Beaton's peculiar sense of humour in his memoirs:

> Sometimes a humorous light comes into his eyes when you tell him something quite ordinary, such as that you have missed your train, and he throws back that graceful head of his and says: 'Oh, I think this is so funny! I think it is the funniest thing I have ever heard,' and you wonder whether he has some strange sub-lunar sense of humour that you cannot follow.

NOEL COWARD

I took to wearing a coloured turtle-necked jersey more for comfort than for effect, and soon I was informed by my evening paper that I had started a fashion ... During the ensuing months I noticed more and more of our seedier West End chorus boys parading about in them.

Noel Coward

Noel Coward, the quintessentially English actor, director, composer, playwright and dandy, rose to fame rapidly. He wrote *The Vortex* in 1924, produced it in London with himself in the leading role, and in 1925 appeared in it on Broadway. Henceforth his versatility was displayed throughout the English-speaking world. His humour – arch, superior and obliquely insolent – depended on lightning rapidity, on situation and contradiction, on a sense of the ridiculous combined with the ability to say the right thing at the right time.

His influence upon his generation was great. 'All sorts of men suddenly wanted to look like Noel Coward,' wrote Cecil Beaton, 'sleek, clipped and well-groomed, with cigarette, telephone or cocktail in hand.' Coward is remembered in this manner as the paragon of style and effortless sophistication. After the success of *The Vortex*, he was photographed in bed wearing a Chinese dressing gown and an expression of terminal *ennui*. By his side were cigarettes and unidentifiable bottles. Silk wraps were draped over the bed, and his head rested on a plump pillow. These photos appeared in *The Sketch* and led to protests from old-fashioned military men complaining that depraved poseurs like Coward would be the downfall of the British Empire.

The dressing gown, of course, became a Coward trademark, but off stage and on the avenue he was a model of almost faultless costume. 'My audition apparel was usually a navy blue suit with a coloured shirt, tie, socks and a handkerchief to match,' he wrote, 'but I had not learnt then that an exact duplication of colours ill becomes the well-dressed man.' Irritated by scruffy dress at rehearsals, he thought that gentlemen should always wear lounge suits. Anything else was not sufficiently enchanting. 'Now I must go and change for dinner,' he said at a cocktail party at his own house in 1944, 'and I shall come down in five minutes' time looking ravishing.'

Coward often featured dandies in his work. In a short story from 1920s called 'Theatre Party', we are introduced to a debonair seducer called Harry Lightfoot. We see him wearing 'his faultless evening dress concealed by a still more faultless coat with a suspicion of velvet at the collar and a carefully knotted white silk scarf enhanced by a tasteful monogram in black'. In 'The Wooden Madonna', a short story written in the 1930s, we meet Aubrey Dakers, a *flâneur* and playwright in search of a plot:

Aubrey Dakers relaxed, a trifle self-consciously, in a pink cane chair outside the Café Bienvenue. He crossed one neatly creased trouser leg over the other and regarded his suede shoes whimsically for a moment and then, lighting a cigarette, gave himself up to the enjoyment of the scene before him.

In his short stories and plays, Coward created an image of the dandy as stylish socialite who does nothing but attend parties and make quips. In doing so, Coward freed dandyism from the philosophical overtones imposed upon it by Baudelaire and Wilde. More importantly, he replaced Brummell's cold impertinence and Huysmans's lethargic decadence with a charming and carefree insouciance, a cocktail cure for the anguish of the Lost Generation.

'Life is nothing but a game of make-believe,' Coward wrote in 1923. 'We none of us ever mean anything,' proclaims a character in the play *Hay Fever*. Coward's dandyism existed for the purpose of amusement. Like life itself, it was not something to be taken too seriously. *In Conversation Piece* (1934), a play set during the Regency, Coward mocked a group of dandy characters in the song 'Regency Rakes':

> We're Regency Rakes
> And each of us takes
> A personal pride
> In the thickness of hide
> That prevents us from seeing
> How vulgar we're being.

Coward was a snob with attitude, but this archetype of upper-class English style started life as an ordinary boy from the suburbs. He grew up in a conventional lower middle class environment, but was relentlessly ambitious and devoted to social climbing. He developed his 'Mayfair' accent and his clipped manner of speech so that he could realise his social aspirations. 'I am related to no one except myself,' he said at the age of twenty-one, but this was simply wishful thinking. His life was full of such paradoxes. Behind the façade of wit lurked a gnawing despair that led to three nervous breakdowns.

It was this difference between appearance and reality that caused Coward to adopt the dandy model of never revealing one's true feelings publicly and always remaining cool-headed. 'His manner created distance between himself and those who would approach him,' remarked one friend. Coward himself described his public and professional persona as 'immense calm with your heart pounding'. Swan-like, Coward appeared to move gracefully and elegantly through society, but below the surface he thrashed his little feet for all he worth just to keep moving.

JAMES BOND

Noel Coward was a good friend of Ian Fleming, and we can detect more than a hint Coward's calm sophistication in Fleming's most famous creation. The spy, dandy and womaniser James Bond was first launched on an unsuspecting public in the early 'fifties, when Fleming wrote *Casino Royale*, *Live and Let Die*, and *Moonraker*, the first three Bond novels. Bond, the last great fictional dandy, has exquisite style. He smokes 'a Balkan and Turkish mixture made for him by Morlands of Grosvenor Street'. He lives in a Chelsea flat, drives 'one of the last 4-litre Bentleys with the supercharger by Amherst Villiers', wears Sea Island cotton shirts, dines at Blade's and kills with a .25 Beretta. In *Moonraker*, Fleming described the simple elegance of Bond's clothes:

> Ten minutes later, in a heavy white silk shirt, dark blue trousers of navy serge, dark blue socks, and well-polished black moccasin shoes, he was sitting at his desk with a pack of cards in one hand and Scarne's wonderful guide to cheating open in front of him.

Entirely the sum of his tastes and material possessions, Bond himself is almost invisible. Perhaps as befits a spy, his true character remains hidden.

On the silver screen, Sean Connery ensured that Bond remained a dandy. Connery was extremely dapper, and his leisurely smile, economy with words, deadpan wit and impassive manner combined to create the perfect Bond.

Noel Coward

Chapter 9
HOW TO GO INTO DECLINE

A career as a dandy is not recommended for a man interested in stability or longevity, as a quick recap of the great dandies will confirm. Ronald Firbank, Ernest Dowson, Saki and Aubrey Beardsley all died young. Arthur Symons and Noel Coward suffered nervous breakdowns. Gérard de Nerval went mad and committed suicide. Brian Howard too killed himself. Thomas Wainewright was deported. Oscar Wilde was imprisoned and died in exile. William Gerhardie faded into obscurity. Lord Alvanley found himself financially ruined. Golden Ball Hughes and Scrope Davies fled England to escape creditors. Lord Byron died abroad. Beau Brummell never did things by halves: he faced financial ruin, fled England, was imprisoned, went mad and died abroad.

Very few dandies found themselves able to grow old gracefully. Harold Acton and Max Beerbohm exiled themselves in China and Italy respectively, away from the social rounds and the public eye. Poodle Byng was mocked as a 'Regency Remnant'. Casanova became a librarian. Edward Bulwer Lytton and Benjamin Disraeli toned down their dandyism and went into politics, safe in the knowledge that an old politician could be respectable where an old dandy would only be risible. The ideal solution, possible only in fiction, is never to grow old, as in *The Picture of Dorian Gray*.

The dandy is a heroic young meteor, a shooting star for whom fatal burn-out is inevitable, an opulent social butterfly whose beauty and grace last only the shortest of seasons. These bright comets flash across the night sky and disappear from view. Tragic though this may seem, their fate is a fact of their existence. And after all, premature death is more fitting to the dandy than premature baldness.

Chapter 10
THE CLASSIC DANDY LOOK

I merely try casually in a hit-and-miss way to dress well.

FRANZ KAFKA

The first key to becoming a dandy is to look like one. This is easier than it sounds. Franz Kafka became a dandy without too much trouble. On 31st December 1911, whilst writing his diary, he remembered his moth-eaten adolescent appearance:

> I naturally noticed – it was obvious – that I was unusually badly dressed, and even had an eye for others who were well dressed, but for years on end my mind did not succeed in recognising in my clothes the cause of my miserable appearance.

He set out to change his appearance by adopting the clothes and personal mannerisms of the dandy and *littérateur*, dressing with refined elegance and frequenting the popular literary clubs, cafés and cabarets of Prague. Photographs from 1900 to 1910 show him looking decidedly foppish, wearing silk neckties, upturned collars, bowlers, and even a top hat, tuxedo and gloves. The Austrian writer Felix Stössinger remembers being fascinated by this tall, elegant *habitué* of Prague's literary cafés. He described Kafka as the 'best dressed man he had ever seen'. Follow Kafka's example and you can't go wrong.

CRAVATS

The cravat has played an important part in the history of dandyism and, although hard to carry off these days, it remains the dandy's talisman. Golden Ball Hughes was famous for inventing the black cravat, as worn by no lesser personage that the great Count D'Orsay, but it was Beau Brummell who undertook the first reform of the neck-cloth. The prevailing cravat of the time was certainly deplorable — enormous, baggy, and often grubby. Brummell dealt with this calamity by inventing the lightly starched muslin cravat. Imitators, of course, always exceed their model, and the other Regency dandies starched their cravats to such an extent that they were unable to move their heads to talk to neighbouring guests at dinner parties. One poor chap had his cravat starched so stiffly that it cut off his ear when he moved his head too quickly.

Brummell soon became notorious for his perfect cravat, but exactly how he tied the thing remained a closely guarded secret. The Prince Regent, eager to discover the key to Brummell's cravat-knotting prowess, once spent an entire morning trying to emulate the Beau's refined technique. Brummell's secret, it seems, was simply that he was rigorous in his quest for perfection. If a recalcitrant cravat did not correspond to his wishes in its first arrangement, it was instantly cast aside in favour of a new one. One of Brummell's friends saw the Beau's valet one morning leaving the great dandy's chamber with an armful of crumpled cravats. 'These are our failures,' the valet commented. A vindictive poet satirised the rite:

My neckcloth of course, forms my principal care,
For by that we criterions of elegance swear,
And costs me, each morning, some hours of flurry,
To make it appear to be tied in a hurry.

DEPORTMENT

She learnt to flash a smile as brilliant as Cedric's own.
'I make her say "brush" before she comes into a room,'
he told me. 'It's a thing I got out of an old book on
deportment and it fixes at once this very gay smile on
one's face. Somebody ought to tell Lord Alconleigh
about it.'

NANCY MITFORD, *Love in a Cold Climate*

Eugene was free, and as a dresser
Made London's dandy his professor.
His hair was fashionably curled,
And now at last he saw the World.
In French Onegin had perfected
Proficiency to speak and write,
In the mazurka he was light,
His bow was wholly unaffected.
The World found this enough to treat
Eugene as clever, and quite sweet.

PUSHKIN, *Eugene Onegin*

In Regency England, slouching was made impossible by
stiffly starched shirts and incredibly tight jackets, often
shaped with whalebone. Breathing was pretty difficult too.
It was *en vogue* to stand bolt upright with a slightly pained
expression on one's face. And then faint.

With the rise of Decadence in the late nineteenth

century, the fashion changed. Standing to attention at social functions was discouraged – indeed, it looked positively out of place when done in the middle of an opium den. Even sitting upright was considered a social *faux pas*. Instead, dandies reclined listlessly in luxurious armchairs and draped themselves over divans and against walls. Their repose became a languid abstraction. The key was to adopt a posture that made the passer-by assume you were waiting to be sculpted. The Decadent posture was a physical manifestation of the *ennui* that afflicted the generation.

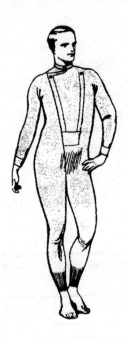

BUTTONHOLES

A really well-made buttonhole is the only link between Art and Nature.

OSCAR WILDE

Reginald slid a carnation of the newest shade into the buttonhole of his latest lounge coat, and surveyed the results with approval. 'I am just in the mood,' he observed, 'to have my portrait painted by someone with an unmistakable future. So comforting to go down to posterity as 'Youth with a Pink Carnation' in catalogue-company with 'Child with a Bunch of Primroses' and all that crowd.'

SAKI, 'THE INNOCENCE OF REGINALD'

It's such a shame that buttonholes are today worn only at weddings. Why men don't wear them on happy occasions, I do not know. In other ages, men wore flowers every day of the week. Oscar Wilde popularised the wearing of a green carnation. In fin-de-siècle England, this unnatural flower came to mean something more than a mere buttonhole. It stood for a brief and brilliant season or two as the symbol of the age, representing a mood rather than a moment: a mood that was at once indolent, voluptuous, bizarre, witty and deliberately artificial.

TIES

The essential thing for a necktie is style. A well-tied tie is the first serious step in life.

OSCAR WILDE

Did the Greeks and Romans wear collars and ties, and if not, why not?

JAMES LAVER

The dandy has a large collection of ties, and he wears them only with a Windsor knot, an invention of the Prince of Wales, later Edward VIII. In the 1920s, the Prince of Wales's invention for neckties was the most fashionable thing in London, but no one seemed to achieve the Prince's giddy heights of brilliance in tying it. When picking the Prince's brain on matters sartorial in 1923, Fred Astaire obtained the secret of that impressively large knot. 'Of course, my dear Astaire, I'll explain how it's done,' said the Prince. The effect, he revealed, required more than a special technique of tying: 'I have my ties cut wider than normal and the extra material creates a bigger knot.'

PETS

Pets are not essential possessions for the dandy, but they have the potential to be amusing diversions, stylish accessories and a way of accentuating your utter difference. When choosing a pet, one must apply the same principles as when choosing an item of clothing. Spend as much time and as much money as you would when buying a new suit. After all, you don't want your sartorial splendour to be sullied by the presence of a mangy and disreputable mongrel at your side.

A number of famous dandies have made exquisite choices in this respect. Poodle Byng, the Regency buck, would never go outside unless accompanied by his pet poodle, which he coiffeured to match his own curly hairstyle. Lord Byron kept a bear, ten horses, six dogs, three monkeys, five cats, an eagle, a parrot, a crow, a falcon and five peacocks. Baudelaire bought a bat, which he kept in a cage on his writing desk. In the 1830s the Parisian poet Gérard de Nerval took his pet lobster for walks on a leash, allowing the lobster to determine both the direction and the pace.

Perhaps we would be better off following the example of Maury Noble, a dandyish character in F. Scott Fitzgerald's novel *The Beautiful and The Damned*, who drags behind him a dead crab tied to a piece of string, often engaging it in long conversations about the applications of the binomial theorem.

The most suitable pet for a dandy is the tortoise. This animal is a perfect *flâneur*, never happier than when meandering slowly through urban environments on a leash. In this respect, the tortoise has the advantage over the lobster, which spends half its time in a bad mood, moping and pining for water whenever you try to walk it on dry land. Furthermore, the tortoise's shell can be painted to match your tie or cravat.

Please ensure that you use a non-toxic paint. Whatever you do, don't encrust your tortoise's shell with jewels. In Huysmans's *A Rebours*, Duc Jean des Esseintes buys a huge tortoise and has its shell glazed with gold and encrusted with precious stones, but with unfortunate results:

> He felt suddenly uneasy about the tortoise. It was lying absolutely motionless. He touched it. It was dead. Accustomed no doubt to a sedentary life, it had not been able to bear the dazzling luxury imposed upon it.

SNUFFBOXES

The Regency dandies were avid takers of snuff, a scented and powdered form of dried tobacco snorted rather inelegantly through the nostrils. In the early nineteenth century, the dandy's enormous collection of snuffboxes was a significant status symbol. Beau Brummell preferred a snuffbox that he could display in his hand to a Raphael that he could exhibit only on his wall. His snuffboxes were numerous and costly. But even in taking snuff he had his style: he always opened the box with one hand, the left.

Lord Petersham, a friend of Golden Ball Hughes and an eccentric dandy, was said to possess a different snuffbox for every day of the year. One day a visitor admired a delightful light blue Sèvres snuffbox. 'Yes,' Petersham lisped in reply, 'it is a nice summer box, but it would not do for winter wear.'

Chapter 11
DANDY ACTIVITIES

The dandy's love of idleness has been spelt out elsewhere in this book, so here perhaps we should refer not to the dandy's activities but to his 'inactivities'. Either way, the question remains the same: how can we best make the day's dour hours dwindle into graceful moments? In part, the riddle solves itself. Idleness makes the hours fly past where work would make them drag their heels. The *flâneur* who kicks back in a café and chats to his companions will find his days pass so quickly that they are gone before he notices.

On occasion, however, we notice the dark cloud of agonising *ennui* creeping in our direction. Immediately we must find some form of diversion to hold boredom at bay. For if work is the dandy's enemy, boredom is his nemesis. It is useful, therefore, to remember the maxim about time flying whenever one is enjoying oneself. The dandy's unbridled soul requires a suitably hedonistic pastime that promises immediate excitement. Reckless gambling and excessive drinking fill the vacant hours better than any bourgeois hobby you may care to note.

But some fellows find that their hearts have become so

accustomed to the pleasures of the lesser sins that their senses are now benumbed and their tastes blunted. Excess seems as pointless as moderation. Like Dorian Gray before them, they find that the grass on the other side of conventional morality appears to be so much greener. The only activities that hold out the promise of charm are entirely disreputable. Cue Raffles, the gentleman thief, creeping across rooftops to steal your jewels.

CONVERSATION

Knowledge makes the gentleman, but 'tis conversation
that completes him.

THOMAS FULLER

Reginald affects an exhaustive knowledge of things
political, which furnishes an excellent excuse for not
discussing them.

SAKI

I have never felt obliged, like Oscar Wilde, to sit down
at a dinner table and hold forth for a couple of hours.
I'm not saying that I couldn't – but oh! how boring for
the poor guests.

NOEL COWARD

Ambrose lived in and for conversation; he rejoiced in
the whole intricate art of it – the timing and striking
the proper juxtaposition of narrative and comment,
the bursts of spontaneous parody, the allusion one
would recognise and one would not, the changes of
alliance, the betrayals, the diplomatic revolutions, the
waxing and waning of dictatorships that could happen
in an hour's session about a table.

EVELYN WAUGH, *Put Out More Flags*

One should never listen. To listen is a sign of indifference to one's hearers.

Oscar Wilde

If I'm in a group of people who are talking about high politics, I have sense enough to keep quiet and listen to them. And if they happen to be talking about finance, I keep much quieter and possibly go to sleep.

Noel Coward

Talk to every woman as if you loved her, and to every man as if he bored you, and at the end of your first season you will have the reputation of possessing the most perfect social tact.

Oscar Wilde

I have observed that the distinguishing trait of people accustomed to good society, is a calm imperturbable quiet, which pervades all their actions and habits, from the greatest to the least; they eat in quiet, move in quiet, live in quiet, and lose their wife, or even their money in quiet; while low persons cannot take up either a spoon or an affront without making such an amazing noise about it.

Edward Bulwer Lytton

Make him laugh and he will think you a trivial fellow, but bore him in the right way and your reputation is assured.

W. SOMERSET MAUGHAM

I love talking about nothing. It's the only thing I know anything about.

OSCAR WILDE, *An Ideal Husband*

'What,' asked my friend, 'makes for good conversation?'

'The impertinence of the man!' I exclaimed. 'You've been talking to me for hours, and yet you suddenly demand to know what makes for good conversation. You sound like you're pining for one.'

'Confound you!' he retorted. 'I'm simply asking your opinion on the matter. I shall rephrase my question. What makes a good conversationalist?'

'Perhaps you can modify it a little further in order to gratify my egotistical desires,' I hinted.

'What makes you such a good conversationalist?' he asked, with a smirk.

'I'm not a sycophant, for a start,' I said.

My companion looked exasperated. 'But I have heard it said that a gossip talks about others, a bore talks about himself, and a brilliant conversationalist talks about you.'

'I'd rather not talk about me,' my friend said. 'I've been having trouble at home, and I don't want to dwell on it. My wife's run off with Lord Egremont's valet.'

'Lord Egremont's valet? He's no better than a common street vendor! The swine!'

'Please, I'd rather not discuss the matter.'

'Certainly,' I said. 'Tell me, perhaps, your theories on conversation.'

'I'm of the opinion that no man would listen to someone else if he didn't know that it was his turn next.'

'You've been labouring under a delusion,' I replied. 'No gentleman ever listens to anyone else. He certainly never listens to himself. It's the height of bad manners. And speaking of turns, I think that the time has come for Lord Egremont's valet to explain himself. Let's go and horsewhip the rascal.'

FLANERIE

For the perfect idler, for the passionate observer it becomes an immense source of enjoyment to establish his dwelling in the throng, in the ebb and flow, the bustle, the fleeting and the infinite.

CHARLES BAUDELAIRE

My former *ennui* had returned and I felt its weight even more heavily than before; I doubted whether further attempts at sociability would ever relieve me of it. What I required was not exactly solitude, but the opportunity to roam around freely, meeting people when I wished and taking leave of them when I wished.

GÉRARD DE NERVAL

The dandy is blasé or feigns to be ... his passions and his profession are to wed himself to the crowd ... The observer is a prince who revels everywhere in his incognito ... he plunges into the crowd as if into an immense reservoir of electricity.

CHARLES BAUDELAIRE

The greater part of men of genius were great *flâneurs*... Often it is at the time when the artist or the poet seems the least occupied in their work, that they are plunged in it the deepest.

THE LAROUSSE DICTIONARY, 1872

When I found myself alone, and in the midst of a crowd, I began to be astonishingly happy ... Among these hurrying people, under the smoky sky, I could walk and yet watch. If there was ever a religion of the eyes, I have devoutly practised that religion. I noted every face that passed me on the pavement; I looked into the omnibuses, the cabs, always with the same eager hope of seeing some beautiful or interesting person ... I grasped at all these sights with the same futile energy as a dog that I once saw standing in an Irish stream, and snapping at the bubbles that ran continually past him on the water. Life ran past me continuously, and I tried to make all its bubbles my own.

ARTHUR SYMONS

The dandy, that divine alien, is always a city dweller. He would not know what to do with himself if he was cut adrift in the countryside. His favourite activity is a quintessentially urban form of loafing known as *flânerie*. The word derives from the French verb *flâner*, which means 'to stroll' or 'to loaf'. *Flânerie*, therefore, is the activity of strolling around town with no particular aim in mind, and the *flâneur* is an urban idler. He can exist only in the metropolis. He ambles down the avenues of time and dawdles on the boulevards of the city, sauntering through life. The pavement is his catwalk, and he poses for the populace, watching the crowd and being watched by the crowd. He delights in being amidst the herd though not of it, and he reaps existential security from this spectacle of the teeming urban population, finding his solitude in the multitude.

Baudelaire was the true chronicler of *flânerie*. The *flâneur*, thought Baudelaire, was the aristocrat of the crowd – his way of living 'still bestowed a conciliatory gleam over the growing destitution of men in the great city.'

Walter Benjamin, the Marxist cultural theorist, planned to write a history of *flânerie*. He visualised it as a collection of notes and quotes on nineteenth-century Paris, and he worked on it for over ten years. In the end, however, it became the Frankenstein's monster of *flânerie* and developed beyond the control of its creator. Benjamin only ever published a small and incomplete section of this sprawling masterpiece, which he called 'The Arcades Project', under the title *Charles Baudelaire: A Lyric Poet in the Era of High Capitalism*.

As Benjamin noted, the arcades – those covered streets flowing with lowlife, low-level consumerism and loafers – were the centre of the universe for the Parisian *flâneurs*. 'It is in this world,' he wrote, 'that the *flâneur* is at home. It provides the favourite sojourn of the strollers and the smokers, the stamping ground of all sorts of little *métiers*, with its chronicler and its philosopher.' From *flânerie* arose the custom of the aperitif and the cocktail hour, window-shopping and the extension of shop opening hours to ten o'clock.

The rise of the *Feuilleton* – the daily newspaper that featured serial novels, city-sketches and short items of news – quickened the rise of *flânerie*. The *flâneur* was henceforth able to maintain the life of a gentleman of leisure whilst earning a modest living from journalism. According to Benjamin, the street-journalist was always on stand-by for work – loitering, dallying and strolling through town: 'The walls are the desk against which he presses his notebooks; news-stands are his libraries and the terraces of cafés are the balconies from which he looks down on his household after his work is done.'

The dandy delights in this vision of easy work. He loves to sit at a table outside a café, daydreaming about life, observing the spectacle of humanity, and occasionally committing his thoughts to paper. He rises to walk down the fashionable streets, swinging his cane as he saunters at an easy pace. Humanity, in turn, may now observe him, and the circle is complete.

CAFE CULTURE

There, in that exuberant vista of gilding and crimson
velvet set amidst all those opposing mirrors and
upholding caryatids, with fumes of tobacco ever rising
to that painted and pagan ceiling, and with the hum of
presumably cynical conversation broken into so sharply
now and again by the clatter of dominoes shuffled on
marble tables, I drew a deep breath, and 'This indeed,'
said I to myself, 'is life!'

Max Beerbohm describing the Café Royal in
'Enoch Soames'

Café society has an illustrious history among gentlemen of
leisure. Then, as indeed now, they were places of repose in
which to see and be seen. At the height of their popularity
in eighteenth-century London, coffee houses were a place
where you could gamble, read, converse, exchange ideas,
show off your newest cane or cravat, read seditious literature, and even drink coffee if you must. As Rose Macaulay
wrote in *Life Among the English*;

> High living and, if not high thinking, at least incessant
> talking, prevailed among the more leisured classes.
> Conversation was ardently pursued; men rose of a
> morning, met at their pet coffee houses, exchanged
> news, and talked; later they went to dinner and still
> talked; then walked and talked in the park or mall, then

to assembly or play and talked more, then again to coffee or chocolate house, where they played and talked until midnight. Young law students would arrive at their coffee house *déshabillés* (gay nightcaps, slippers, dressing gowns and sashes) newspapers in hand, and 'saunter away the time' admiring one another's get-up; "the vain things approached each other with an air that shows they regard one another for their vestments".'

By the end of the nineteenth century, the Café Royal on Regent Street, modelling its mood from the beautiful world of Parisian café society frequented by Baudelaire, was the place to be seen. Decadent dandies about town, including Wilde and Beardsley, frequented that 'haunt of daring and intellect' – the domino room.

DRINKING

A glass of absinthe is as poetical as anything in the world. What difference is there between a glass of absinthe and a sunset?

Oscar Wilde

Whiskey and beer are for fools. Absinthe has the power of the magicians; it can wipe out or renew the past, and annul or foretell the future.

Ernest Dowson

One must be drunk always.

Charles Baudelaire

I have discovered that alcohol taken in sufficient quantities produces all the effects of drunkenness.

Oscar Wilde

The dandy never drinks beer. Pint glasses look so ugly in his manicured hand. He chooses only those drinks that can be seen as refined, exotic or obscure. Champagne, favoured by Ronald Firbank, must be drunk in large quantities. Absinthe comes highly recommended. Drink absinthe and you will be in the company of Zola, Baudelaire, Wilde, Rimbaud, Voltaire, Toulouse-Lautrec and Degas. Verlaine sung the praises of absinthe in his youth and damned it on his deathbed. Paul Gauguin and Van Gogh drank absinthe together when they shared accommodation in 1888. Due to excessive absinthe consumption, Van Gogh turned out to be the flatmate from hell, as Gauguin's diary illustrates:

> He ordered a light absinthe. Suddenly he flung the glass and its contents into my face. I managed to duck and grab him ... a few minutes later, Vincent was in his own bed ... not to awaken until morning. When he awoke he was perfectly calm and said to me: My dear Gauguin, I have a dim recollection that I offended you last night.

Three days later, on Christmas Eve, Van Gogh chased Gauguin down the street with a razor. That night, Van Gogh cut off his own ear whilst under the influence of absinthe.

Anthony Blanche in *Brideshead Revisited* countenances the drinking of 'real G-g-green Chartreuse, made before the expulsion of the monks. There are five distinct tastes as it trickles over the tongue. It is like swallowing a sp-spec-trum'. In *The Great Gatsby*, Jay Gatsby has a collection of 'gins and liquors and cordials so long forgotten that most of his female guests were too young to know one from another.'

Cocktails too are essential. The Dry Martini, of course, is rather suave — indeed, nothing associated with James Bond could be anything but. In *Casino Royale*, Bond describes his perfect cocktail, a variation on the theme. 'Three measures of Gordon's, one of vodka, half a measure of Kina Lillet,' he tells the barman. 'Shake it very well until it's ice cold, then add a large thin slice of lemon peel … This drink's my own invention. I'm going to patent it when I can think of a good name'. The CIA agent Felix Leiter suggests that Bond call it the 'Molotov Cocktail'.

The best thing about cocktails is the ritual involved in their making, and gadgets can be a cocktail connoisseur's best friends. Jay Gatsby has 'a machine in the kitchen which could extract the juice of two hundred oranges in half an hour if a little button was pressed two hundred times by a butler's thumb.' The butler, on the other hand, should never be a cocktail connoisseur's best friend.

GAMBLING

Much was drunk, much money spilt at cards, dice and prize-fights. Wagering was incessant; it might be on a fight, a cock, a political event, an amorous affair, or the pace of a four-in-hand to Brighton.

ROSE MACAULAY ON THE REGENCY DANDIES IN
Life Among the English

I have a notion that Gamblers are as happy as most people, being always excited. Women, wine, fame, the table, even Ambition, sate now and then; but every turn of the card, and even the cast of the dice, keeps the Gamester alive.

LORD BYRON

In *Casino Royale*, Ian Fleming tells us that James Bond had always been a gambler: 'He loved the dry riffle of the cards and the constant unemphatic drama'. Bond is simply one in a long line of gambling dandies. In Regency London, the gambling clubs thrived as a result of the dandies' insatiable passion to get rid of their money. These clubs, located in St James's, became the exclusive haunts of the fashionable man-about-town. Membership of White's, the most exclusive gambling club of all, was the supreme social distinction. A contemporary observer called it 'the club from which people have died of exclusion, killed on the spot by a black ball.'

Gambling in White's was extreme. On one occasion, a man walked through the front door and immediately collapsed. Within seconds, bets were taken as to whether he was dead or merely unwell. Down the road from White's was Crockford's, where dandies took tremendous chances gambling at Hazard, a dice game of pure chance similar to the modern American game of craps. The club's manager, a retired fishmonger known as 'Old Crocky', was said to have won by one means or another the disposable income of the entire Regency generation.

Gambling often had dire results. The arch-dandy Lord Alvanley was a member of White's, and he gambled recklessly, leading to the break-up of the family estates. Beau Brummell, Scrope Davies and Golden Ball Hughes gambled away their fortunes and fled to Paris to escape their creditors.

HORSE-RIDING

Driving had become a craze, and young bucks gaily spanked round town and parks in curricles, phaeton or gigs behind fine horses and got up to kill.

Rose Macaulay on the Regency dandies in
Life Among the English

In Regency England, the dandies were noted for their love of horses. The thought of sitting in an ornate carriage behind two or more of these proud animals appealed to their sense of innate nobility. Pierce Egan's famous *Life in London*, published in 1821, features a couple of athletic Regency bucks called Jerry Hawthorn and Corinthian Tom. In their 'rambles and sprees through the Metropolis', these two eccentrics love nothing more than driving a pair of horses at breakneck speed through the back streets of London.

In the early nineteenth century, the dandies would go riding in Rotten Row in Hyde Park. 'Where else can we see such beautiful women, such gallant cavaliers, and such fine horses?' asked Disraeli. Hyde Park was still rural in this Golden Age. Cows and deer grazed under its green trees. It was the dandy's paradise – especially, said Disraeli, 'at the end of a long sunny morning in the merry month of May'. Captain Gronow recalled it with nostalgia: 'You did not see any of the lower or middle classes of London intruding themselves into this region which, with a sort of tacit understanding, was then given up exclusively to persons of rank and fashion.'

By the time of the Regency, horse racing was firmly established as an aristocratic sport. When the Jockey Club was founded in the middle of the eighteenth century, its avowed aim was to enable the dandies 'to hold their own against the rabble ... without more intrusion than was absolutely necessary on the part of the profane and vulgar.'

When English dandyism moved to France after the Napoleonic war, the French dandies followed their English counterparts by making the horse their most fashionable accessory. But the French got too overexcited to maintain any sense of decorum. The horse became more than fashionable – it became essential. The French dandy spent every waking moment either riding a horse, or driving a carriage behind a pair of horses, or betting on horse racing – and he talked about nothing but horses.

The sport of driving – once defined as the art of remaining alive in a carriage built for display rather than for locomotion – returned to France with the Restoration, the aristocratic carriages having been burnt in the Revolution some years before. The French dandies began their own society to keep the peasants out of horse racing – and they called it Le Jockey Club.

DISREPUTABLE DEEDS

Dandies are not known for being moral creatures. They tend to live by their own laws and morals. Hedonism, after all, is not a virtuous philosophy. Some dandies, however, are more immoral than others. One dandy in particular is renowned for taking pleasure in crime. Raffles, the gentleman thief created by E. W. Hornung, is not afraid of transgressing the bounds of legality. The Raffles stories first appeared in *The Strand* and a few other British magazines during the 1890s. Wearing either a dinner jacket or 'one of his innumerable blazers', Raffles creeps across rooftops and picks locks with the skill of an expert locksmith, vanishing into the night with hoards of diamonds and gold.

He appears to be 'rich enough to play cricket all the summer, and do nothing for the rest of the year', but Raffles is in fact 'a little hard up':

> Do you think that because a fellow has rooms in this place, and belongs to a club or two, and plays a little cricket, he must necessarily have a balance at the bank? I tell you, my dear man, that at this moment I'm as hard up as you ever were. I have nothing but my wits to live on – absolutely nothing else.

'Why should I work when I could steal?' he asks, but the issue is not that simple. Raffles steals at least as much for the pleasure of demonstrating his skill as for monetary benefit. Furthermore, there is 'a fine streak of aestheticism in his complex composition' – so he steals only beautiful items of jewellery. We see him steal 'rings by the dozen, diamonds by the score; bracelets, pendants, aigrettes, necklaces, pearls, rubies, amethysts, sapphires; and diamonds always, diamonds in everything, flashing bayonets of light.'

Chapter 12
THE DANDY'S LEGACY:
THE GODFATHER OF
POP

The future belongs to the dandy. It is the exquisites who are going to rule.

OSCAR WILDE

Now you've read about the dandy, his laws, his attitudes and heard brave tales of the greatest exponents of the art. Yet you still ask the question, what relevance does this cane-wielding, cravat-wearing anachronism have in the twenty-first century?

Well, dear pupil, as I've tried to impress upon you all along, the dandy is an eternal creature who has little to do with the dress of any particular era and everything to do with timeless attitude and style, a desire to self-promote and rebel against a prevailing order and fashion it in his own divine image.

The dandy didn't, as you might think, die out after the Second World War. On the contrary, he simply popped up somewhere new and unexpected and rose to greater prominence than ever before as the driving force behind the spectacular rise of pop culture and the subcultures that slowly began to announce themselves from the streets. Amid the blurring of traditional class distinctions, the dandy was reborn as the rebellious style prince of the proles.

The steady increase in leisure time and disposable income for the working classes meant that for the first time its youth had a stage on which to voice what it thought of the world and play out their differences from it. From the black American zoot suit wearing gangs of the 1940s to the immaculate styling of British mods in the 1960s it was the tried and tested tenets of dandyism that these pop sub-cultures used in their guerilla war of rebellion through style.

The following description of zoot suit hipster style from Malcolm X's autobiography shows that the rituals and codes of twentieth-century youth culture could be just as wonderfully ridiculous as anything found at the height of nineteenth-century dandyism:

> I was measured, and the young salesman picked off a rack a zoot suit that was just wild: sky-blue pants thirty inches in the knee and angle-narrowed down to twelve inches at the bottom, and a long coat that pinched my waist and flared out below my knees. As a gift, the salesman said, the store would give me a narrow leather belt with my initial on it. Then he said I ought to buy a hat, and I did – blue, with a feather in the four-inch brim. Then the store gave me another

present: a long, thick-lined, gold-plated chain that swung down lower than my coat hem ... I took three of those twenty-five-cent sepia-toned, while-you-wait pictures of myself, posed the way 'hipsters' wearing their zoots would 'cool it' – hat angled, knees drawn close together, feet wide apart, both index fingers jabbed towards the floor.

Similarly the mods took style to absurd extremes that would make Brummell proud. Assimilating their favourite aspects of modernist continental European and urban American culture, they drove around town – like Regency bucks in the Row – on Italian scooters, drank espresso, wore Italian suits, watched French films, and listened to black American R 'n' B.

Colin MacInnes's novel *Absolute Beginners* describes the mod protagonist, known as The Dean: 'college-boy smooth cropped hair with burned-in parting, neat white Italian rounded-collar shirt, short Roman jacket very tailored (two little vents, three buttons), no-turn-up narrow trousers with 17-inch bottoms absolute maximum, pointed-toe shoes and a white mac lying folded by his side.'

As dandies firmly within the Beau Brummell tradition, mods cultivated a highly refined aesthetic sensibility, pushed often to the point of fetish. Although they revelled in the new consumer age, for the mods it always was more important to exhibit good taste than affluence – 'better to have one perfect suit than a dozen with the wrong number of buttons,' as one commentator has noted.

In truth you can take any subculture of the post-war era – they're all dandies at heart. The beatniks of the 1950s and the hippies in the 1960s were a return to the eastern, ethnic and romantic obsessions of nineteenth-century bohemian dandies. While the glam rockers and punks that succeeded them and turned ideas of taste on their head wanted nothing more than society to view them as aliens from another world. Whether composed of the finest tailoring Italy had to offer or rags held together by safety pins these pop dandies always wore their sartorial pomp like regal peacocks secure in the knowledge that for at least a moment they were It.

So if you think that the dandy died out with cravats and silver canes, think again. His time has finally come, he is truly the man of the age. In our seemingly classless era – where we are now judged not by what we do but by what we consume – style and attitude are the new gods. Surely only the dandy, with his guile and innate poise, is naturally equipped to survive and prosper.

Appendix:
A BRIEF NOTE ON THE ORIGIN OF THE WORD 'DANDY'

The origin of the word 'dandy' is shrouded in mystery, obscured by the mists of time, but there are two distinct possibilities with regard to its genesis. According to the first theory, the word moved from France to Scotland in the sixteenth century and thence to England. The French word *dandin*, meaning 'nincompoop' or 'fool' was transferred from France to Scotland in 1548 along with tens of thousands of French soldiers in the war against England. The meaning then mutated, and the word began to be used not as a term of abuse but as a term of grudging respect. By the 1750s, the term 'Jack-a-Dandy' was used on the Scottish border to mean 'rake' or 'cad'.

The second possibility is that the word is English in origin and that the date of its first use is even earlier. The word 'dandiprat' or 'dandyprat' was used in the 1490s to refer to the silver half-groat of Henry VII. An edition of The *Northampton Mercury* dated 17th April 1819 reported as follows: 'This term ... appears to have arisen from a small silver coin struck by Henry VII, of little value, called a dandiprat; and hence Bishop Fleetwood observes the term is applied to worthless and contemptible persons.' Bishop Fleetwood, incidentally, wouldn't have known what 'style' was if it had leapt up and slapped him in his chubby face. Worthless and contemptible persons indeed!

Index